Cooking Light

slow cooker tonight!

Cooking Light.
slow cooker
tonight!

Oxmoor House.

ISBN-13: 978-0-8487-3657-6
ISBN-10: 0-8487-3657-5
Library of Congress Control Number: 2012942587

Printed in the United States of America
First Printing 2012

Be sure to check with your health-care provider before making any changes in your diet.

Oxmoor House

VP, Publishing Director: Jim Childs
Editorial Director: Leah McLaughlin
Creative Director: Felicity Keane
Brand Manager: Michelle Turner Aycock
Managing Editor: Rebecca Benton

Cooking Light Slow Cooker Tonight!

Senior Editor: Heather Averett
Assistant Designer: Allison Sperando Potter
Director, Test Kitchen: Elizabeth Tyler Austin
Assistant Directors, Test Kitchen: Julie Christopher, Julie Gunter
Recipe Developers and Testers: Wendy Ball, RD; Victoria E. Cox; Stefanie Maloney; Callie Nash; Leah Van Deren
Recipe Editor: Alyson Moreland Haynes
Food Stylists: Margaret Monroe Dickey, Catherine Crowell Steele
Photography Director: Jim Bathie
Senior Photo Stylist: Kay E. Clarke
Photo Stylist: Katherine Eckert Coyne
Assistant Photo Stylist: Mary Louise Menendez
Production Manager: Theresa Beste-Farley

Contributors

Project Editor: Perri Hubbard
Recipe Developers and Testers: Martha Condra, Tamara Goldis, Erica Hopper, Kathleen Royal Phillips
Copy Editors: Jacqueline Giovanelli, Jasmine Hodges
Proofreader: Tara Trenary
Indexer: Mary Ann Laurens
Nutritional Analyses: Wendy Ball, RD; Keri Matherne, RD
Interns: Erin Bishop; Mackenzie Cogle; Jessica Cox, RD; Laura Hoxworth; Susan Kemp; Anna Pollock; Ashley White
Photographers: Johnny Autry, Beau Gustafson, Beth Hontzas, Mary Britton Senseney
Photo Stylists: Mindi Shapiro Levine, Lydia DeGaris Pursell

Time Home Entertainment Inc.

Publisher: Richard Fraiman
Vice President, Strategy & Business Development: Steven Sandonato
Executive Director, Marketing Services: Carol Pittard
Executive Director, Retail & Special Sales: Tom Mifsud
Director, Bookazine Development & Marketing: Laura Adam
Executive Publishing Director: Joy Butts
Finance Director: Glenn Buonocore
Associate General Counsel: Helen Wan

Cooking Light ®

Editor: Scott Mowbray
Creative Director: Carla Frank
Executive Managing Editor: Phillip Rhodes
Executive Editor, Food: Ann Taylor Pittman
Special Publications Editor: Mary Simpson Creel, MS, RD
Senior Food Editors: Timothy Q. Cebula, Julianna Grimes
Senior Editor: Cindy Hatcher
Assistant Editor, Nutrition: Sidney Fry, MS, RD
Assistant Editors: Kimberly Holland, Phoebe Wu
Test Kitchen Director: Vanessa T. Pruett
Assistant Test Kitchen Director: Tiffany Vickers Davis
Recipe Testers and Developers: Robin Bashinsky, Adam Hickman, Deb Wise
Art Directors: Fernande Bondarenko, Shawna Kalish
Senior Deputy Art Director: Rachel Cardina Lasserre
Designers: Hagen Stegall, Dréa Zacharenko
Assistant Designer: Nicole Gerrity
Photo Director: Kristen Schaefer
Assistant Photo Editor: Amy Delaune
Senior Photographer: Randy Mayor
Senior Photo Stylist: Cindy Barr
Photo Stylist: Leigh Ann Ross
Chief Food Stylist: Kellie Gerber Kelley
Food Styling Assistant: Blakeslee Wright
Copy Chief: Maria Parker Hopkins
Assistant Copy Chief: Susan Roberts
Research Editor: Michelle Gibson Daniels
Production Director: Liz Rhoades
Production Editor: Hazel R. Eddins
Assistant Production Editor: Josh Rutledge
Administrative Coordinator: Carol D. Johnson
CookingLight.com Editor: Allison Long Lowery
Nutrition Editor: Holley Johnson Grainger, MS, RD
Associate Editor/Producer: Mallory Daugherty Brasseale

To order additional publications, call
1-800-765-6400 or 1-800-491-0551

For more books to enrich your life, visit
oxmoorhouse.com

To search, savor, and share thousands
of recipes, visit **myrecipes.com**

Cover: Company Pot Roast (page 56)
Back cover: Red Beans and Rice (page 84), Barley, Black Bean, and Corn Burritos (page 169), Amaretti Cheesecake (page 259), Potato Soup (page 185), Spicy Chicken Stew (page 216), and Garlic Chicken (page 131)

introduction

For delicious make-ahead meals, nothing beats a slow cooker. Perfect for hectic weeknights, it's the only tool you'll need to transform simple ingredients and lean cuts of meat into filling, flavorful meals—so you can serve your family slow-simmered goodness without spending hours over the cooktop.

Here, we've compiled 140 of our all-time favorite recipes for the ultimate slow-cooker collection. Try **Company Pot Roast** (page 56) for a comforting classic, or **Chicken and Shrimp Jambalaya** (page 149) for a zesty crowd-pleaser with a Cajun kick. You'll also find fresh flavors and vegetarian options to shake up your dinnertime routine, such as **Thyme-Scented White Bean Cassoulet** (page 171) or **Curried Squash and Apple Soup** (page 197). Even better, this book can take you beyond the slow-cooker standbys with recipes like refreshing **Berry-Lemonade Tea** (page 27) or irresistibly gooey **Brownie Pudding Cake** (page 263).

But because you want more than just a collection of recipes, we've also included a Cooking Class (page 8) with the most valuable information about this handy appliance. Brimming with our best techniques and tips, it will guide you through every step of the process, from finding the right slow cooker to simplifying cleanup.

With *Cooking Light Slow Cooker Tonight!*, our dedicated staff of culinary professionals and registered dietitians gives you all the tools and recipes at your fingertips to prepare healthful, satisfying slow-cooker meals any night of the week. Let these kitchen-tested recipes breathe new life into your slow cooker—tonight!

The *Cooking Light* Editors

contents

5   Introduction

8   Cooking Class

16   Appetizers & Beverages

42   Meats

118   Poultry

162   Meatless Main Dishes

182   Soups & Stews

224   Sides, Condiments & Desserts

270   Nutritional Analysis

271   Metric Equivalents

272   Index

cooking class

A slow cooker is a busy cook's best friend. Follow our tips and techniques to ensure a wholesome, delicious meal every time you use this convenient appliance.

Benefits of Slow Cooking

In addition to allowing you to make meals ahead, your slow cooker offers these benefits:

• **Cleans up easily**—Usually you have only one container to wash (assuming you don't brown or sauté ingredients in a skillet before adding them to your cooker), or no container if you use heavy-duty plastic liners.

• **Environmentally friendly**—A slow cooker uses less electricity than the cooktop or oven. There's no extra heat escaping, so your kitchen stays cool.

• **Requires little attention**—You don't have to stand over a hot cooktop or watch the clock. The slow cooker works best when it's left alone to slowly simmer food.

• **Adaptable**—Most traditional recipes that call for long, slow, gentle cooking in a Dutch oven are adaptable to the slow cooker. Some of your family's favorite recipes can be ready when you walk through the door at the end of a hectic day.

• **Economical**—Tough, less-expensive cuts of meat transform into tender, moist, and richly flavored dishes when cooked in the slow cooker.

• **Healthier**—Seldom do you add fat when cooking meat or poultry in the slow cooker. During the long simmering time, any fat rises to the top of the cooking liquid; simply remove it before serving.

• **Portable and versatile**—You can position the slow cooker any place there's an electrical outlet. It's especially useful when you entertain or have limited counter space. Prepare hot drinks and appetizers in the slow cooker, and place the cooker where your guests will gather. Just make sure to use the LOW setting.

Best Cuts of Meat for Slow Cooking

Type of Meat (3 ounces cooked)	Calories	Fat (sat)
Chuck or rump roast	206	13.1g (4.9g)
Tip roast	199	11.3g (4.3g)
Lean beef stew meat	201	9.6g (3.6g)
Lean Boston butt roast	197	12.2g (4.4g)
Lamb stew meat	158	6.2g (2.2g)

Shopping for a Slow Cooker

With so many slow cookers on the market, it's hard to know which one to buy. Here are some tips to help you get started.

Size matters. The first thing to consider when selecting a slow cooker is which best suits your family. If you are cooking for yourself or a family of two, then a 3- to 4-quart size should work for you. Families of four or larger should look at a 5- or 6-quart slow cooker. Or, if you love to have leftovers, a 6-quart cooker is a good selection.

Keep a lid on it. A snug-fitting, see-through lid works best. Removing the cooker's lid during cooking releases a great deal of heat, so you want to be able to see the food through the lid.

Removable inserts. Slow cookers with removable inserts are easier to clean than one-piece units. Depending on the manufacturer, the insert may be dishwasher safe. Some inserts can go from the freezer to the cooker, and some can even be used to brown meat on the cooktop before slow cooking.

It's all in the timing. Many slow cookers come with programmable timers. This is an especially nice feature if you will be gone all day. If your slow cooker doesn't have one, purchase an external timer. Simply plug the external slow-cooker timer into the wall outlet, and then plug the cooker into the timer. It allows you to set the cooking time; when that time expires, the timer will automatically switch the cooker to warm.

Slow-Cooker Showdown

We tested our Provençal Beef Daube recipe (page 200) in six slow cookers—all with at least a 6-quart capacity—ranging in price from $35 to a hefty $280. The results varied more in appearance and flavor than anticipated. In our favorite cookers, the meat was more tender and succulent, and the cooking liquid was rich and well blended. In other cookers, flavors were less deliciously integrated. Our conclusion: The more successful pots seemed to cook at a slightly higher temp—even on the LOW settings, the stews bubbled a bit as they simmered.

Best Overall:

BREVILLE BSC560XL 7-QUART ($180)
Although this stainless cooker lacks a timer and operates with manual controls, it produced great results. We loved the lightweight cooking insert; it's safe for the cooktop. This model also includes a meat rack and a long, detachable cord. One drawback: A metal lid might tempt you to peek.

Best Value:

WEST BEND 84966 6-QUART ($80)
A close second, this model has a digital timer. The cooking insert is safe for cooktop use, and the warming element doubles as a griddle, so you can cook directly on it. There are three heat settings: HIGH, LOW, and WARM, a nice feature for entertaining or for families who eat in shifts.

Secrets of Slow Cooking

On a budget? Pressed for time? Transform tough, cheap cuts into delicious dinners that practically cook themselves. Try our top tips.

Tip #1: Brown Meat First for Better Flavor

Strictly speaking, meat doesn't need to be browned before it's added to the slow cooker, but it's a step we find worth the effort. The caramelized surface of the meat will lend rich flavor to the finished dish. And meat dredged in flour before browning will add body to the sauce (as in Provençal Beef Daube, page 200). Always brown and drain ground meat before putting it in the slow cooker. Otherwise, it may clump and add grease to the dish.

Tip #2: Spice Judiciously

Whole spices and dried herbs like cinnamon sticks, bay leaves, caraway seeds, and peppercorns will give intense flavor to a dish that cooks for several hours, so be careful not to overdo them. Chopped fresh herbs such as parsley remain vibrant if you stir them in near the end or when the dish is finished.

Tip #3: Use Less Liquid

Because the slow cooker generates steam that doesn't escape, there will be more liquid in the food when it's finished cooking than when it started. If you create or adapt a recipe for the slow cooker, decrease (by as much as half) the amount of liquid you normally use in the dish.

Tip #4: Know When to Go HIGH, and When to Go LOW

Generally, cooker temperatures range from 170° to 280°. Use the HIGH setting if you need to cook a more tender cut of meat relatively quickly. But for tougher cuts, it's best to use the LOW setting and cook longer to allow time for the meat to become tender.

Tip #5: Leave the Lid On!

Don't lift the lid until the dish is done. The steam generated during slow cooking is part of the cooking medium. Removing the lid will release this steam and increase cooking time. Moreover, when you lift the lid, temperatures can drop into the "danger zone" (between 40° and 140°) where bacteria multiply rapidly.

Tip #6: Account for Variables

Our Test Kitchen professionals find that some slow cookers—particularly some newer models—cook hotter than others. In one instance, liquid imperceptibly evaporated from the cooker, leaving far less sauce than when the same dish was prepared in a different model. Not all slow cookers are created equal, so don't rely on the stated cook time for a recipe until you know how your cooker behaves.

Our Test Kitchen's Top Slow-Cooker Tricks

1. Make-ahead magic. If your slow cooker has a removable insert, you can assemble the ingredients for some recipes in the insert the night before, and then refrigerate the whole thing. Starting with cold ingredients may increase the cook time.

2. Don't get burned. Although cooking time is more flexible in a slow cooker than in an oven, overcooking is possible, so test for doneness close to the time given in the recipe.

3. Remember time conversions. One hour on HIGH equals approximately 2 hours on LOW.

4. Cut uniform pieces. When cutting meat or vegetables, be sure the pieces are the same size so they cook evenly.

5. Trim the fat. Slow cooking requires little fat. Trim excess fat and skin from meats and poultry.

6. Add, don't stir. There's no need to stir ingredients unless a recipe specifically calls for it. Just layer the ingredients as the recipe directs.

7. You won't need much liquid; use only the amount of liquid specified in a recipe.

8. Lay it on thick. You can thicken the juices and make gravy by removing the lid and cooking on HIGH for the last 20 to 30 minutes.

9. Finish fresh. To enhance the flavor, add seasonings and garnishes to the dish once it comes out of the slow cooker.

Slow-Cooker Safety

Slow cooking is a safe method for preparing food if you follow the standard procedures.

• Fill your slow cooker at least half full but no more than two-thirds full. This helps meat products reach a safe internal temperature quickly and cook evenly.

• If the recipe calls for browning the meat first, you can forgo the HIGH setting for the first hour. Precooking the meat jump-starts the initial temperature of the ingredients, eliminating the safety risk associated with slow cooking raw meats.

• Defrost any frozen foods before cooking a dish that includes meat, poultry, or seafood. This ensures that the contents of the insert reach a safe internal temperature quickly.

• Don't use your slow cooker to reheat leftovers, because the cooker will not heat the food fast enough, resulting in an increased risk of bacterial contamination. Instead, use a microwave or cooktop.

Quick Cleanup

Follow these tips to make cleaning your slow cooker a little easier.

• To minimize cleanup, buy clear, heavy-duty plastic liners made to fit 3- to 6½-quart oval and round slow cookers. Place the plastic liner inside the slow cooker before adding the recipe ingredients. Then, serve the meal directly from the slow cooker, with the liner in place. Once the cooker has cooled, just throw away the plastic liner along with the mess.

• If you don't have slow-cooker liners, be sure to coat the slow cooker with cooking spray before placing the food inside. This will make cleanup much easier.

• The best time to clean a slow-cooker insert is not long after you take the food out, once the insert has cooled slightly. Just make sure that the slow cooker isn't too hot. Cold water poured over a hot insert can cause it to crack.

• Never immerse a slow-cooker unit in water. Simply unplug it, and wipe it clean with a cloth.

appetizers
&beverages

Hot Mulled Ginger-Spiced Cider

By preparing this cider in an electric slow cooker, you free up the cooktop. However, you can also heat it in a pot on the stove, if you prefer.

Yield: 12 servings (serving size: 1 cup)

3 whole cloves

2 (4 x 1–inch) strips orange rind

2 whole allspice

1 (3-inch) cinnamon stick

1 (½-inch) piece peeled fresh ginger

12 cups apple cider

½ cup apple jelly

¼ teaspoon ground nutmeg

1. Place first 5 ingredients on a 5-inch-square double layer of cheesecloth. Gather edges of cheesecloth together; tie securely.

2. Place cheesecloth bag, cider, jelly, and nutmeg in an electric slow cooker. Cover and cook on HIGH for 4 hours. Remove and discard cheesecloth bag.

3. Ladle cider into mugs.

CALORIES 174; FAT 0g; PROTEIN 1g; CARB 43.8g; FIBER 0g; CHOL 0mg; IRON 0mg; SODIUM 0mg; CALC 0mg

Ginger-Lemon Hot Toddies

Ginger infuses this lemony hot toddy with spiciness—the perfect antidote to chilly winter weather. After you add the alcohol, turn the slow cooker to LOW and allow guests to help themselves.

Yield: 14 servings (serving size: about 1 cup)

8 cups water

2 cups fresh lemon juice (about 14 small lemons)

2 cups honey

5 tablespoons finely chopped crystallized ginger

1 (3-inch) piece peeled fresh ginger, cut into ¼-inch-thick slices

¾ cup golden rum

¾ cup brandy

Lemon rind strips (optional)

1. Place first 5 ingredients in a 4½-quart electric slow cooker. Cover and cook on HIGH for 4 hours. Remove and discard ginger slices.
2. Stir in rum and brandy. Ladle mixture into mugs, and garnish with lemon rind strips, if desired.

CALORIES 226; FAT 0g; PROTEIN 0.5g; CARB 45.6g; FIBER 0.1g; CHOL 0mg; IRON 0.3mg; SODIUM 7mg; CALC 10mg

Spiced Caramel Cider

If you'd prefer a beverage with less spice, try substituting apple juice for the apple cider. It's fantastic either way.

Yield: 12 servings (serving size: about 1 cup)

½ cup sugar

3 tablespoons water

1 tablespoon butter

⅓ cup whipping cream

5 whole allspice

5 whole cloves

2 (3-inch) cinnamon sticks

10 cups apple cider

¼ cup fresh orange juice

1 tablespoon fresh lemon juice

Cinnamon sticks (optional)

1. Place sugar and 3 tablespoons water in a small, heavy saucepan over medium-low heat. Cook 3 minutes or until sugar melts, stirring gently. Continue cooking 5 minutes or until golden (do not stir). Remove from heat; let stand 1 minute. Add butter, stirring until melted. Gradually add whipping cream, stirring constantly. Cook over medium heat 1 minute or until caramel sauce is smooth, stirring constantly. Remove from heat.

2. Place allspice, cloves, and cinnamon sticks on a double layer of cheesecloth. Gather edges of cheesecloth together; tie securely. Place in a 4-quart electric slow cooker. Add cider, orange juice, and caramel sauce, stirring until caramel sauce dissolves. Cover and cook on LOW for 3 hours. Remove and discard cheesecloth bag. Stir in lemon juice.

3. Ladle cider into mugs. Garnish with cinnamon sticks, if desired.

CALORIES 180; FAT 3g (sat 1.9g, mono 0.9g, poly 0.1g); PROTEIN 1g; CARB 38.4g; FIBER 0g; CHOL 10mg; IRON 0mg; SODIUM 9mg; CALC 6mg

Mocha Hot Chocolate

Serve this coffee-flavored hot chocolate with a batch of your favorite biscotti.

Yield: 9 servings (serving size: ⅔ cup)

1 (1½-quart) container chocolate light ice cream

3 cups 2% reduced-fat milk

2 tablespoons instant espresso granules

1. Spoon ice cream into a 3-quart electric slow cooker. Add milk and espresso. Cover and cook on LOW for 3 hours or until thoroughly heated.

2. Ladle hot chocolate into mugs.

CALORIES 187; FAT 6.3g (sat 3.7g, mono 1.5g, poly 0.2g); PROTEIN 6.7g; CARB 25.1g; FIBER 1.3g; CHOL 33mg; IRON 0mg; SODIUM 93mg; CALC 175mg

Berry-Lemonade Tea

Here's a refreshingly fruity mix of tea and lemonade that is delicious hot or cold—depending on the season. You can even spike it!

Yield: 12 servings (serving size: 1 cup tea and 1 lemon slice)

12 regular-sized tea bags

8 cups water

5 cups refrigerated natural lemonade

⅓ cup honey

1 (12-ounce) package frozen mixed berries

2 lemons, each cut into 6 slices

1. Remove paper tags from tea bags. Place tea bags, 8 cups water, and next 3 ingredients (through berries) in a 5-quart electric slow cooker. Cover and cook on LOW for 3 hours.

2. Pour tea through a sieve into a bowl; discard solids. Serve warm or over ice. Garnish with lemon slices.

CALORIES 87; FAT 0.1g; PROTEIN 0.3g; CARB 23.4g; FIBER 0.8g; CHOL 0mg; IRON 0.1mg; SODIUM 6mg; CALC 5mg

Cheesy–Spinach Crab Dip

This cheesy crab dip makes a savory party appetizer with minimal preparation time. Serve warm with pita chips or whole-grain crackers.

Yield: 20 servings (serving size: ¼ cup)

1½ cups lump crabmeat, drained and shell pieces removed

4 ounces shredded 50% reduced-fat jalapeño cheddar cheese, (about 1 cup)

3 ounces grated fresh Parmesan cheese (about ¾ cup)

½ cup fat-free milk

½ cup grated onion (about ½ large onion)

½ cup canola mayonnaise

1 tablespoon sherry vinegar

½ teaspoon ground red pepper

2 garlic cloves, minced

1 (10-ounce) package frozen chopped spinach, thawed, drained, and squeezed dry

1 (8-ounce) tub fat-free cream cheese

1 (8-ounce) carton fat-free sour cream

1 teaspoon grated lemon rind

1. Place first 12 ingredients in a 3-quart electric slow cooker; stir well. Cover and cook on LOW for 2 hours. Stir in lemon rind.

CALORIES 118; FAT 6.9g (sat 1.7g, mono 3.3g, poly 1.4g); PROTEIN 9.6g; CARB 4.1g; FIBER 0.9g; CHOL 26mg; IRON 0.4mg; SODIUM 300mg; CALC 165mg

FLAVOR TIP

For those who like their dips hot and spicy, increase the ground red pepper or add crushed red pepper for an additional kick.

Roasted Garlic–White Bean Dip

This white bean dip gets its flavor from a combination of roasted garlic, rosemary, and kalamata olives and its smooth texture from ricotta cheese. If time allows, pick up a baguette and make your own crostini at home, or just serve with crackers.

Yield: 15 servings (serving size: ¼ cup)

¼ cup olive oil

6 garlic cloves, thinly sliced

2 (15.5-ounce) cans cannellini beans, rinsed and drained

⅓ cup water

1 cup fat-free ricotta cheese

3 ounces grated fresh Parmesan cheese (about ¾ cup)

1 teaspoon chopped fresh rosemary

¼ teaspoon freshly ground black pepper

¼ cup pitted kalamata olives, coarsely chopped

½ teaspoon grated lemon rind

Chopped fresh rosemary (optional)

Freshly ground black pepper (optional)

1. Heat a small saucepan over low heat. Add oil to pan; swirl to coat. Add garlic; cook 5 minutes. Place beans and ⅓ cup water in a food processor. Add garlic mixture, ricotta cheese, and next 3 ingredients (through ¼ teaspoon black pepper); process until smooth.

2. Place bean mixture in a 3-quart electric slow cooker. Cover and cook on LOW for 2 hours.

3. Stir in olives and lemon rind. Garnish with rosemary and pepper, if desired.

CALORIES 129; FAT 6g (sat 1.4g, mono 3.8g, poly 0.5g); PROTEIN 7.5g; CARB 11g; FIBER 2.7g; CHOL 7mg; IRON 0.9mg; SODIUM 249mg; CALC 138mg

Blue Cheese–Artichoke Dip

Blue cheese amps up the flavor for a little twist on the traditional artichoke appetizer. The dip holds up well for about two hours after the cook time. Serve with pita chips or toasted baguette slices.

Yield: 20 servings (serving size: ¼ cup)

1 cup chopped onion

¾ cup chopped red bell pepper

1 garlic clove, minced

4 ounces blue cheese, crumbled (about 1 cup)

¼ teaspoon freshly ground black pepper

2 (14-ounce) cans artichoke hearts, drained and coarsely chopped

1 (8-ounce) block fat-free cream cheese, softened

1 (8-ounce) carton reduced-fat sour cream

1. Heat a medium nonstick skillet over medium-high heat. Add onion and bell pepper; sauté 5 minutes. Add garlic; sauté 1 minute. Remove from heat.

2. Place onion mixture in a 2½-quart electric slow cooker. Add blue cheese and remaining ingredients; stir until blended. Cover and cook on LOW for 2 hours or until cheese melts and mixture is thoroughly heated, stirring occasionally.

CALORIES 76; FAT 3.3g (sat 1.9g, mono 0.7g, poly 0.1g); PROTEIN 4.8g; CARB 7.7g; FIBER 3.7g; CHOL 12mg; IRON 0.3mg; SODIUM 188mg; CALC 99mg

INGREDIENT TIP

If you really love blue cheese, then pull out all the stops and choose Gorgonzola for this dip. Among blues, Gorgonzola is moist, creamy, savory, earthy, and slightly spicier than its relatives. However, any blue will do.

Gruyère-Bacon Dip

Serve this dip with assorted vegetable dippers. It's also tasty as a condiment spread on turkey burgers.

Yield: 16 servings (serving size: 2 tablespoons)

½ cup chopped onion

Cooking spray

4 ounces shredded Gruyère cheese (about 1 cup)

½ cup canola mayonnaise

1 teaspoon Worcestershire sauce

½ teaspoon dry mustard

⅛ teaspoon freshly ground black pepper

1 (8-ounce) block fat-free cream cheese, softened

2 tablespoons chopped green onions

4 center-cut bacon slices, cooked and crumbled

1. Heat a large nonstick skillet over medium-high heat. Add onion to pan; sauté 5 minutes or until tender. Remove from heat.

2. Place onion in a 2½-quart electric slow cooker coated with cooking spray. Add cheese and next 5 ingredients (through cream cheese). Stir until blended. Cover and cook on LOW for 1½ hours or until cheese melts, stirring after 45 minutes. Top with green onions and bacon.

CALORIES 102; FAT 8.3g (sat 2.1g, mono 3.9g, poly 1.7g); PROTEIN 4.9g; CARB 1.7g; FIBER 0.1g; CHOL 13mg; IRON 0.1mg; SODIUM 198mg; CALC 124mg

Buffalo-Style Drummettes with Blue Cheese Dip

Heating the chicken drummettes in the oven helps to brown them. You can also brown them, in batches, in a skillet on the cooktop.

Yield: 15 servings (serving size: 2 drummettes, about 1 tablespoon dip, 2 carrot sticks, and 2 celery sticks)

Cooking spray

3 pounds chicken wing drummettes, skinned (30 drummettes)

¼ teaspoon freshly ground black pepper

¾ cup thick hot sauce

2 tablespoons cider vinegar

1 teaspoon reduced-sodium Worcestershire sauce

2 garlic cloves, minced

Blue Cheese Dip

30 carrot sticks

30 celery sticks

1. Preheat oven to 450°.
2. Line a jelly-roll pan with foil; coat foil with cooking spray. Place chicken on prepared pan; sprinkle with pepper. Lightly coat chicken with cooking spray. Bake, uncovered, at 450° for 7 minutes or until lightly browned.
3. Combine hot sauce and next 3 ingredients (through garlic) in an oval 4-quart electric slow cooker coated with cooking spray.
4. Remove chicken from pan; drain on paper towels. Place chicken in slow cooker, tossing gently to coat with sauce. Cover and cook on HIGH for 3 hours or until chicken is very tender. Serve with Blue Cheese Dip, carrot sticks, and celery sticks.

CALORIES 95; FAT 4.8g (sat 1.7g, mono 1.6g, poly 0.7g); PROTEIN 7.9g; CARB 4.4g; FIBER 0.5g; CHOL 25mg; IRON 0.4mg; SODIUM 248mg; CALC 42mg

Blue Cheese Dip

Yield: 18 servings (serving size: about 1 tablespoon)

4 ounces ⅓-less-fat cream cheese (about ½ cup)

½ cup fat-free sour cream

2 tablespoons canola mayonnaise

2 garlic cloves, minced

3 tablespoons blue cheese, crumbled and divided

1. Place cream cheese in a medium bowl; beat with a mixer until smooth. Add sour cream, mayonnaise, garlic, and half of blue cheese, beating until smooth.
2. Stir in remaining blue cheese.

CALORIES 38; FAT 3.1g (sat 1.2g, mono 1.1g, poly 0.4g); PROTEIN 1.1g; CARB 1.5g; FIBER 0g; CHOL 6.9mg; IRON 0mg; SODIUM 62mg; CALC 24mg

Lamb Meatballs

Lemon zest adds a nice bright lift to the spicy sauce and complements the Greek-inspired flavors of these meatballs.

Yield: 14 servings (serving size: 2 meatballs and about 2 tablespoons sauce)

¼ cup grated onion, drained

¼ cup dried currants

½ teaspoon ground cumin

¼ teaspoon ground allspice

¼ teaspoon ground cinnamon

¼ teaspoon crushed red pepper

2 garlic cloves, minced

1 large egg

2 tablespoons chopped fresh mint

½ pound ground lamb

½ pound ground turkey

¾ cup fresh breadcrumbs

1 tablespoon olive oil

Cooking spray

1 (24-ounce) jar spicy red pepper pasta sauce

1 teaspoon grated lemon rind

1. Combine first 9 ingredients in a large bowl. Add lamb, turkey, and breadcrumbs; stir well. Shape into 28 (1-inch) meatballs.

2. Heat a large skillet over medium-high heat. Add oil to pan; swirl to coat. Add meatballs to pan. Cook 2 minutes on each side or until browned. Transfer meatballs to a 4-quart electric slow cooker coated with cooking spray.

3. While meatballs cook, combine pasta sauce and lemon rind in a medium bowl. Pour sauce over meatballs. Cover and cook on HIGH for 2 hours or until meatballs are done.

CALORIES 134; FAT 6.3g (sat 2.1g, mono 2.3g, poly 0.4g); PROTEIN 9.6g; CARB 10g; FIBER 1.3g; CHOL 37mg; IRON 0.7mg; SODIUM 190mg; CALC 31mg

Salsa Cheesecake

Served with baked tortilla chips, this festive appetizer will be a hit at your next party.

Yield: 20 servings (serving size: 1 cheesecake wedge)

Cooking spray

1 tablespoon dry breadcrumbs

1 (8-ounce) tub light cream cheese with chives and onions, softened

1 (8-ounce) tub fat-free cream cheese, softened

½ cup bottled medium salsa

1 tablespoon all-purpose flour

2 teaspoons chili powder

1 teaspoon ground cumin

1 (4.5-ounce) can chopped green chiles, undrained

1 large egg

1 large egg white

2 ounces preshredded reduced-fat 4-cheese Mexican blend cheese (about ½ cup)

4 cups hot water

¼ cup chopped fresh cilantro

¼ cup chopped seeded tomato

3 tablespoons sliced green onions

3 tablespoons chopped yellow bell pepper

1. Coat a 7-inch springform pan with cooking spray; sprinkle breadcrumbs over bottom of pan. Wrap bottom and sides of prepared pan with foil.

2. Beat cream cheeses with a mixer at medium speed until smooth. Add salsa and next 4 ingredients (through chiles); beat just until blended. Add egg and egg white; beat just until blended (do not overbeat). Stir in Mexican blend cheese. Pour cheese mixture into prepared pan.

3. Place a 10-ounce custard cup or ramekin, upside down, in a round 5-quart electric slow cooker. Place springform pan on top of custard cup. Carefully pour 4 cups hot water into slow cooker, being careful not to get water into cheese mixture. Place several layers of paper towels over top of slow cooker. Cover and cook on HIGH for 1 hour and 45 minutes or until cheesecake is set.

4. Turn slow cooker off. Uncover; discard paper towels (do not remove pan from crockery insert). Carefully run a knife around edge of cheesecake. Remove crockery insert from slow cooker. Let cheesecake stand, uncovered, in crockery insert 30 minutes.

5. Remove pan from crockery insert, and let cheesecake cool completely in pan on a wire rack. Cover and chill 24 hours.

6. Carefully remove sides from springform pan. Layer cilantro, tomato, green onions, and yellow bell pepper in center of cheesecake. Cut into wedges.

CALORIES 56; FAT 2.7g (sat 1.6g, mono 0.7g, poly 0.1g); PROTEIN 4.4g; CARB 3.2g; FIBER 0.4g; CHOL 19.5mg; IRON 0.2mg; SODIUM 212mg; CALC 85mg

meats

Moroccan Meatballs in Spicy Tomato Sauce

Seasoned meatballs simmer in an aromatic tomato sauce for a Mediterranean-style dinner. Use kitchen shears to coarsely chop the tomatoes while they are still in the can. You can shape the meatballs in advance and store them in the freezer to save time. The rest of the recipe is best prepared and cooked the same day.

Yield: 6 servings (serving size: 5 meatballs, 1 cup sauce, and ½ cup couscous)

Meatballs:

½ cup dry breadcrumbs

¼ cup dried currants

¼ cup finely chopped onion

½ teaspoon salt

½ teaspoon ground cumin

½ teaspoon dried oregano

¼ teaspoon ground cinnamon

1½ pounds lean ground beef

1 large egg white

Sauce:

¼ cup tomato paste

1 teaspoon fennel seeds

1 teaspoon grated orange rind

½ teaspoon ground cumin

¼ teaspoon ground cinnamon

¼ teaspoon salt

¼ teaspoon ground red pepper

1 (28-ounce) can whole tomatoes, coarsely chopped

Remaining ingredients:

3 cups hot cooked couscous

Chopped fresh parsley (optional)

1. To prepare meatballs, combine first 9 ingredients in a bowl; shape meat mixture into 30 meatballs. Heat a large nonstick skillet over medium-high heat. Add half of meatballs to pan; cook 3 minutes or until browned, stirring frequently. Place browned meatballs in an electric slow cooker. Repeat procedure with remaining 15 meatballs.

2. To prepare sauce, combine tomato paste and next 7 ingredients (through tomatoes). Add to slow cooker, stirring gently to coat. Cover and cook on LOW for 6 hours. Serve over couscous. Garnish with parsley, if desired.

CALORIES 312; FAT 6g (sat 2.2g, mono 2.2g, poly 0.9g); PROTEIN 28.7g; CARB 37.8g; FIBER 4.2g; CHOL 60mg; IRON 4.6mg; SODIUM 696mg; CALC 85mg

Beef Burgundy with Egg Noodles

For the red wine, try a Chianti or zinfandel. The beef mixture tastes even better after it's been refrigerated a day or two, and then reheated.

Yield: 8 servings (serving size: about 1¼ cups beef mixture, ½ cup egg noodles, and 1½ teaspoons thyme)

2 pounds lean beef stew meat

6 tablespoons all-purpose flour (about 1¾ ounces)

2 cups (1-inch-thick) slices carrot

1 (16-ounce) package frozen pearl onions, thawed

1 (8-ounce) package mushrooms, stems removed

2 garlic cloves, minced

¾ cup fat-free, lower-sodium beef broth

½ cup dry red wine

¼ cup tomato paste

1½ teaspoons salt

½ teaspoon dried rosemary

¼ teaspoon dried thyme

½ teaspoon freshly ground black pepper

8 ounces uncooked egg noodles

¼ cup chopped fresh thyme

1. Place beef in a large bowl; sprinkle with flour, tossing well to coat. Place beef mixture, carrot, onions, mushrooms, and garlic in an electric slow cooker. Combine beef broth and next 6 ingredients (through pepper); stir into beef mixture. Cover and cook on LOW for 8 hours.

2. Cook noodles according to package directions, omitting salt and fat. Serve beef mixture over noodles; sprinkle with thyme.

CALORIES 357; FAT 9.3g (sat 3.3g, mono 3.8g, poly 0.7g); PROTEIN 28.4g; CARB 38.9g; FIBER 2.5g; CHOL 94mg; IRON 4.7mg; SODIUM 637mg; CALC 53mg

Italian Beef Sandwiches

If you can't find Italian rolls, look for a sturdy bread that will soak up the juices in this moist, delightfully messy sandwich.

Yield: 8 servings (serving size: 1 sandwich and about ⅓ cup cooking liquid)

1 teaspoon dried Italian seasoning

1 teaspoon crushed red pepper

1 (2½-pound) rump roast, trimmed

1 (14-ounce) can fat-free, lower-sodium beef broth

1 garlic clove, minced

2 teaspoons olive oil

1 cup coarsely chopped green bell pepper (about 1 medium)

8 (2-ounce) Italian rolls

Giardiniera (pickled vegetables), chopped (optional)

1. Combine first 5 ingredients in a large zip-top plastic bag, and marinate in refrigerator overnight.

2. Place beef and marinade in an electric slow cooker; cover and cook on LOW for 8 hours or until beef is tender. Place beef on a cutting board (reserve cooking liquid); let stand 10 minutes. Thinly slice beef; place in a shallow dish. Pour cooking liquid over beef.

3. Heat a large nonstick skillet over medium-high heat. Add oil to pan; swirl to coat. Add bell pepper to pan; sauté 5 minutes or until tender. Slice rolls lengthwise, cutting to, but not through, other side. Hollow out top and bottom halves of rolls, leaving a ¾-inch-thick shell; reserve torn bread for another use. Arrange about 3 ounces beef and 2 tablespoons bell peppers on each roll. Drizzle 1 tablespoon cooking liquid over beef and peppers; top with giardiniera, if desired. Serve with remaining 2½ cups cooking liquid for dipping.

CALORIES 386; FAT 11.3g (sat 3.4g, mono 4.8g, poly 1.2g); PROTEIN 39.4g; CARB 29.2g; FIBER 1.8g; CHOL 102mg; IRON 5.4mg; SODIUM 479mg; CALC 52mg

Beef Stroganoff

You probably have many of these ingredients on hand. Just shop for the meat and mushrooms for an easy family meal. Garnish with fresh dill, if desired.

Yield: 4 servings (serving size: about 1 cup stroganoff and ½ cup noodles)

1 (1-pound) top round steak (1 inch thick), trimmed

1 cup chopped onion

2 tablespoons chopped fresh parsley

2 tablespoons Dijon mustard

½ teaspoon salt

½ teaspoon dried dill

½ teaspoon freshly ground black pepper

1 (8-ounce) package sliced mushrooms (about 2 cups)

3 garlic cloves, minced

1.5 ounces all-purpose flour (about ⅓ cup)

1 cup fat-free, lower-sodium beef broth

1 (8-ounce) carton reduced-fat sour cream

2 cups hot cooked medium egg noodles (about 4 ounces uncooked noodles)

1. Cut steak diagonally across grain into ¼-inch-thick slices. Place steak, onion, and next 7 ingredients (though garlic) in a 3-quart electric slow cooker; stir well.

2. Weigh or lightly spoon flour into a dry measuring cup; level with a knife. Place flour in a small bowl; gradually add broth, stirring with a whisk until blended. Add broth mixture to slow cooker; stir well. Cover and cook on HIGH for 1 hour. Reduce heat to LOW, and cook for 7 to 8 hours or until steak is tender. Turn slow cooker off; remove lid. Let stroganoff stand 10 minutes. Stir in sour cream. Serve stroganoff over noodles.

CALORIES 454; FAT 15.8g (sat 7.5g, mono 4.9g, poly 0.6g); PROTEIN 36.5; CARB 40.3g; FIBER 2.8g; CHOL 126mg; IRON 4.4mg; SODIUM 691mg; CALC 127mg

Curried Beef Short Ribs

Finishing this dish with lime zest and juice brightens its rich flavors. Round out your meal with some baby bok choy, if desired.

Yield: 6 servings (serving size: about 3 ounces meat, ⅔ cup rice, and about 2½ tablespoons sauce)

2 teaspoons canola oil

2 pounds beef short ribs, trimmed

½ teaspoon kosher salt, divided

¼ teaspoon freshly ground black pepper, divided

⅓ cup minced shallots

3 tablespoons minced garlic

3 tablespoons minced peeled fresh ginger

¼ cup water

2 tablespoons red curry paste

¼ cup light coconut milk

1 tablespoon sugar

1 tablespoon fish sauce

1 teaspoon grated lime rind

1 tablespoon fresh lime juice

4 cups hot cooked basmati rice

1. Heat a large nonstick skillet over medium-high heat. Add oil to pan; swirl to coat. Sprinkle ribs with ¼ teaspoon salt and ⅛ teaspoon pepper. Add half of ribs to pan; cook 2 minutes on each side or until browned. Place ribs in an electric slow cooker. Repeat procedure with remaining ribs.

2. Add shallots, garlic, and ginger to pan; sauté 2 minutes. Stir in ¼ cup water and curry paste; cook 1 minute. Stir in coconut milk, sugar, and fish sauce. Add coconut milk mixture to slow cooker. Cover and cook on LOW for 6 hours.

3. Remove ribs from slow cooker; keep warm. Strain cooking liquid through a colander over a bowl; discard solids. Place a zip-top plastic bag inside a 2-cup glass measure. Pour cooking liquid into bag; let stand 10 minutes (fat will rise to the top). Seal bag; carefully snip off 1 bottom corner of bag. Drain cooking liquid into a small bowl, stopping before fat layer reaches opening; discard fat. Stir in remaining ¼ teaspoon salt, remaining ⅛ teaspoon pepper, rind, and juice. Remove meat from bones. Shred meat with 2 forks; discard bones. Serve sauce over meat and rice.

CALORIES 446; FAT 17.8g (sat 7.2g, mono 7.7g, poly 1g); PROTEIN 32.5g; CARB 36.6g; FIBER 0.6g; CHOL 89mg; IRON 4.8mg; SODIUM 585mg; CALC 26mg

WINE TIP

The intense flavor of Curried Beef Short Ribs will overwhelm most wines. Reach for a fruit-forward red.

Beef Brisket with Beer

Beef brisket is at its finest when you simmer it in a slow cooker and flavor it with beer and onions.

Yield: 12 servings (serving size: about 3 ounces brisket and ⅓ cup sauce)

1 (3-pound) beef brisket, trimmed

1 teaspoon salt

½ teaspoon freshly ground black pepper

¼ cup water

2 cups vertically sliced onion (about 1 large)

1½ cups chopped parsnip (about 2)

1 tablespoon balsamic vinegar

1 bay leaf

1 (12-ounce) bottle light beer

1. Rub brisket with salt and pepper. Heat a large heavy skillet over medium-high heat. Add brisket to pan; cook 10 minutes, browning on all sides. Remove brisket from pan. Add ¼ cup water to pan, stirring to loosen browned bits. Add onion and parsnip; sauté 5 minutes or until vegetables are tender.

2. Place onion mixture, vinegar, bay leaf, and beer in a large electric slow cooker. Place brisket on top of onion mixture. Cover and cook on LOW for 8 hours. Discard bay leaf. Cut brisket diagonally across grain into thin slices. Serve brisket with sauce.

CALORIES 160; FAT 5g (sat 1.9g, mono 2.1g, poly 0.2g); PROTEIN 20.5g; CARB 5.6g; FIBER 1.1g; CHOL 49mg; IRON 1.9mg; SODIUM 232mg; CALC 20mg

QUICK TIP

Round out your meal with a quick addition of creamy mashed potatoes. Prepackaged refrigerated potatoes are a good choice. Just be careful to watch the serving size, and pay close attention to the sodium.

Company Pot Roast

Dried shiitake mushrooms can replace the morels. Leftover meat and gravy make a delicious filling for hot roast beef sandwiches the next day.

Yield: 8 servings (serving size: 3 ounces roast, 1 onion wedge, about 3 carrot pieces, 4 potato halves, and about ¼ cup gravy)

1 (2-pound) boneless chuck roast, trimmed and cut in half

¼ cup lower-sodium soy sauce

2 garlic cloves, minced

1 cup beef broth

1 (0.35-ounce) package dried morels

1 tablespoon cracked black pepper

3 tablespoons sun-dried tomato paste

2 medium onions (about ¾ pound), quartered

1 (16-ounce) package carrots, cut into 2-inch pieces

16 small red potatoes (about 2 pounds), halved

1 tablespoon canola oil

1½ tablespoons all-purpose flour

3 tablespoons water

Rosemary sprigs (optional)

1. Combine roast, soy sauce, and garlic in a large zip-top plastic bag; seal bag, and marinate in refrigerator at least 8 hours, turning bag occasionally.

2. Bring broth to a boil in a small saucepan; add mushrooms. Remove from heat; cover and let stand 20 minutes. Drain mushrooms through a cheesecloth-lined colander over a bowl, reserving broth mixture.

3. Remove roast from bag, reserving marinade. Sprinkle roast with pepper, gently pressing pepper into roast. Combine reserved marinade, mushroom broth mixture, and tomato paste; stir well, and set aside.

4. Place mushrooms, onion, carrot, and potato in a 6-quart electric slow cooker; toss gently.

5. Heat a large skillet over medium-high heat. Add oil to pan; swirl to coat. Add roast, browning well on all sides. Place roast over vegetables in slow cooker. Pour tomato paste mixture into pan, scraping pan to loosen browned bits. Pour tomato paste mixture over roast and vegetables. Cover and cook on HIGH for 1 hour. Reduce heat to LOW, and cook for 8 hours or until roast is tender. Place roast and vegetables on a serving platter; keep warm. Reserve liquid in slow cooker; increase heat to HIGH.

6. Place flour in a small bowl. Gradually add 3 tablespoons water, stirring with a whisk until well blended. Add flour mixture to liquid in slow cooker. Cook, uncovered, 15 minutes or until slightly thick, stirring frequently. Serve gravy with roast and vegetables. Garnish with rosemary sprigs, if desired.

CALORIES 318; FAT 6.8g (sat 1.6g, mono 2.7g, poly 0.8g); PROTEIN 30.5g; CARB 33.1g; FIBER 5.2g; CHOL 40mg; IRON 3.9mg; SODIUM 552mg; CALC 70mg

Beef Pot Roast with Turnip Greens

Cipollini onions are small, flat Italian onions. If you can't find them, substitute pearl onions. Other large, full-flavored greens like mustard greens or kale will work as well.

Yield: 12 servings (serving size: 3 ounces roast, ¾ cup vegetable mixture, and ⅓ cup cooking liquid)

3.4 ounces all-purpose flour (about ¾ cup)

1 (3-pound) boneless chuck roast, trimmed

1 teaspoon kosher salt

½ teaspoon freshly ground black pepper

1 tablespoon olive oil

1 pound fresh turnip greens, trimmed and coarsely chopped

3 cups (2-inch) diagonally cut parsnips (about 1 pound)

3 cups cubed peeled Yukon gold potatoes (about 1 pound)

2 cups cipollini onions, peeled and quartered

2 tablespoons tomato paste

1 cup dry red wine

1 (14-ounce) can fat-free, lower-sodium beef broth

1 tablespoon black peppercorns

4 thyme sprigs

3 garlic cloves, crushed

2 bay leaves

1 bunch fresh flat-leaf parsley

Thyme sprigs (optional)

1. Place flour in a shallow dish. Sprinkle beef evenly with salt and pepper; dredge in flour. Heat a large skillet over medium-high heat. Add oil to pan; swirl to coat. Add beef; cook 10 minutes, browning on all sides. Place turnip greens in a 6-quart electric slow cooker; top with parsnip, potato, and onion. Transfer beef to slow cooker. Add tomato paste to skillet; cook 30 seconds, stirring constantly. Stir in wine and broth; bring to a boil, scraping pan to loosen browned bits. Cook 1 minute, stirring constantly. Pour broth mixture into slow cooker.

2. Place peppercorns and next 4 ingredients (through parsley) on a double layer of cheesecloth. Gather edges of cheesecloth together; tie securely. Add cheesecloth bundle to slow cooker. Cover and cook on LOW for 8 hours or until beef and vegetables are tender. Remove and discard cheesecloth bundle. Remove roast from slow cooker; slice. Serve with vegetable mixture and cooking liquid. Garnish with thyme sprigs, if desired.

CALORIES 424; FAT 21.3g (sat 8.1g, mono 9.4g, poly 0.9g); PROTEIN 33g; CARB 23.5g; FIBER 2.9g; CHOL 99mg; IRON 3.8mg; SODIUM 348mg; CALC 90mg

Slow-Simmered Meat Sauce with Pasta

Mafaldine is a flat noodle with ruffled edges; you can substitute spaghetti, if you like.

Yield: 8 servings (serving size: 1 cup pasta, 1 cup sauce, 1 tablespoon basil, and 2 tablespoons cheese)

1 tablespoon olive oil

2 cups chopped onion

1 cup chopped carrot

6 garlic cloves, minced

2 (4-ounce) links hot Italian sausage, casings removed

1 pound ground sirloin

½ cup kalamata olives, pitted and sliced

¼ cup no-salt-added tomato paste

1½ teaspoons sugar

1 teaspoon kosher salt

½ teaspoon crushed red pepper

1 (28-ounce) can no-salt-added crushed tomatoes, undrained

1 cup no-salt-added tomato sauce

1 tablespoon chopped fresh oregano

16 ounces uncooked mafaldine pasta

½ cup torn fresh basil

3 ounces shaved fresh Parmigiano-Reggiano cheese

1. Heat a large skillet over medium-high heat. Add oil to pan; swirl to coat. Add onion and carrot to pan; sauté 4 minutes, stirring occasionally. Add garlic; cook 1 minute. Place vegetable mixture in a 6-quart electric slow cooker. Add sausage and beef to pan; cook 6 minutes or until browned, stirring to crumble. Remove beef mixture from pan with a slotted spoon. Place beef mixture on a double layer of paper towels; drain. Add beef mixture to slow cooker. Add olives and next 6 ingredients (through tomato sauce) to beef mixture in slow cooker, stirring to combine. Cover and cook on LOW for 8 hours. Stir in oregano.

2. Cook pasta according to package directions, omitting salt and fat. Serve sauce with hot cooked pasta; top with basil and cheese.

CALORIES 503; FAT 16.7g (sat 5.7g, mono 8g, poly 2g); PROTEIN 26.3g; CARB 59.7g; FIBER 5.6g; CHOL 48mg; IRON 4.8mg; SODIUM 766mg; CALC 198mg

Brazilian Feijoada

Feijoada (pronounced fay-ZWAH-da), a Brazilian stew of pork and black beans, is traditionally served over rice with fresh orange slices for special occasions. Preparing it in a slow cooker makes it possible to serve on even the busiest weeknights.

Yield: 8 servings (serving size: about 1¼ cups bean mixture and 1 orange wedge)

2 cups dried black beans

4 applewood-smoked bacon slices

1 (1-pound) boneless pork shoulder (Boston butt), trimmed and cut into ½-inch cubes

¾ teaspoon salt, divided

½ teaspoon freshly ground black pepper, divided

3 bone-in beef short ribs, trimmed (about 2 pounds)

3 cups finely chopped onion (about 2 medium)

1¼ cups fat-free, lower-sodium chicken broth

4 garlic cloves, minced

1 (9-ounce) smoked ham hock

1 tablespoon white vinegar

8 orange wedges

1. Place beans in a small saucepan; cover with cold water. Bring to a boil; cook 2 minutes. Remove from heat; cover and let stand 1 hour. Drain.

2. Cook bacon in a large skillet over medium heat until crisp. Remove bacon from pan; crumble. Reserve drippings in pan. Sprinkle pork evenly with ⅛ teaspoon salt and ¼ teaspoon pepper. Increase heat to medium-high. Add pork to drippings in pan; cook 8 minutes, browning on all sides. Transfer pork to a 6-quart electric slow cooker. Sprinkle ribs evenly with ⅛ teaspoon salt and remaining ¼ teaspoon pepper. Add ribs to pan; cook 3 minutes on each side or until browned. Place ribs in slow cooker. Add drained beans, remaining ½ teaspoon salt, onion, and next 3 ingredients (through ham hock) to slow cooker, stirring to combine. Cover and cook on LOW for 8 hours or until beans and meat are tender.

3. Remove ribs from slow cooker; let stand 15 minutes. Remove meat from bones; shred meat with 2 forks. Discard bones. Discard ham hock. Return beef to slow cooker. Stir in vinegar and crumbled bacon. Serve with orange wedges.

CALORIES 458; FAT 17.4g (sat 6.8g, mono 6.7g, poly 1.1g); PROTEIN 39.5g; CARB 35.8g; FIBER 11.6g; CHOL 96mg; IRON 6.4mg; SODIUM 533mg; CALC 102mg

Bolognese

Spoon this savory Italian meat sauce over any pasta of your choice. We love the long, ribbon-style pappardelle.

Yield: 6 servings (serving size: about ¾ cup)

1¾ cups chopped onion

⅔ cup chopped celery

½ cup finely chopped carrot

6 garlic cloves, minced

½ pound ground beef, extra lean

½ pound lean ground pork

½ pound ground veal

1½ cups canned crushed tomatoes

1 cup dry red wine

1 cup lower-sodium beef broth

¼ cup chopped fresh parsley

2 tablespoons tomato paste

2 teaspoons sugar

1 teaspoon dried thyme

1 teaspoon freshly ground black pepper

½ teaspoon dried oregano

¼ teaspoon ground cinnamon

¼ teaspoon salt

1 bay leaf

1. Heat a large nonstick skillet over medium-high heat. Add onion, celery, carrot, and garlic to pan; sauté 4 minutes. Add beef, pork, and veal to vegetable mixture. Cook 5 minutes or until browned; stir to crumble. Drain meat mixture; place in a 6-quart electric slow cooker. Stir in tomatoes and remaining ingredients. Cover and cook on LOW for 8 hours. Remove and discard bay leaf.

CALORIES 241; FAT 7.7g (sat 3g, mono 1.7g, poly 0.4g); PROTEIN 24.6g; CARB 14.4g; FIBER 3g; CHOL 79mg; IRON 2.4mg; SODIUM 365mg; CALC 62mg

FREEZER TIP

The beauty of bolognese? It freezes well. Make it ahead to have on hand for busy weeknights.

Thai Red Curry Beef

Jalapeño seeds add a slight kick to this Thai beef dish. If you want to decrease the heat, seed the jalapeño before mincing.

Yield: 8 servings (serving size: about ¾ cup beef mixture, ½ cup rice, and 1 tablespoon basil)

2 pounds lean beef stew meat

⅛ teaspoon salt

2 cups finely chopped onion (1 onion)

4 garlic cloves, minced

¾ cup lower-sodium beef broth

1 tablespoon dark brown sugar

3 tablespoons red curry paste

2 tablespoons fish sauce

2 tablespoons fresh lime juice

1 (13.5-ounce) can light coconut milk

1 jalapeño pepper, minced

2 cups bagged baby spinach leaves

4 cups hot cooked jasmine rice

½ cup fresh basil leaves

1. Heat a large nonstick skillet over medium-high heat. Add beef; cook 5 minutes or until browned, stirring occasionally. Drain. Place beef in a 4-quart electric slow cooker; sprinkle with salt.

2. Return pan to medium-high heat. Add onion and garlic; sauté 5 minutes or until tender. Spoon onion mixture over beef. Combine beef broth and next 6 ingredients (through jalapeño); pour over beef. Cover and cook on LOW for 6 hours.

3. Stir in spinach. Cover and cook on LOW for 15 minutes or just until spinach wilts. Serve beef mixture over rice; sprinkle with basil leaves.

CALORIES 245; FAT 5.5g (sat 2.3g, mono 2g, poly 0.2g); PROTEIN 27.4g; CARB 20g; FIBER 1.3g; CHOL 50mg; IRON 2.8mg; SODIUM 624mg; CALC 42mg

Sauerbraten

The spicy-sweet gingersnaps soften the tang of white vinegar. Serve the tender marinated beef and sauce over spaetzle (tiny noodles or dumplings) for an authentic German feast.

Yield: 7 servings (serving size: 3 ounces roast and 6 tablespoons sauce)

1 cup water

2 tablespoons sugar

¾ cup white vinegar

1½ teaspoons salt

6 black peppercorns

5 whole cloves

3 bay leaves

1 lemon, sliced

1 (3-pound) rump roast, trimmed

1½ cups sliced onion (1 large)

15 gingersnaps, crumbled

Chopped fresh parsley (optional)

1. Place first 8 ingredients in a large heavy-duty zip-top plastic bag; seal bag. Turn bag to blend marinade. Place roast and onion in bag; seal bag, turning to coat. Marinate in refrigerator 24 hours, turning bag occasionally.

2. Remove roast from marinade, reserving marinade. Place roast in a 5-quart electric slow cooker. Strain reserved marinade through a sieve into a bowl, reserving 1½ cups; discard remaining liquid and solids. Pour 1½ cups strained marinade over roast. Cover and cook on LOW for 5 hours or until roast is tender.

3. Remove roast from slow cooker; cover and keep warm. Add gingersnap crumbs to liquid in slow cooker. Cover and cook on LOW for 8 minutes or until sauce thickens; stir with a whisk until smooth. Serve sauce with roast. Garnish with parsley, if desired.

CALORIES 202; FAT 5.6g (sat 1.7g, mono 2.2g, poly 0.3g); PROTEIN 20.7g; CARB 16.1g; FIBER 0.8g; CHOL 45mg; IRON 2.3mg; SODIUM 512mg; CALC 30mg

Pork with Apricots, Dried Plums, and Sauerkraut

Sauerkraut balances the sweetness of the apricot preserves and orange juice. Slow cooking tenderizes the pork and dried fruit.

Yield: 8 servings (serving size: 3 ounces pork and about ½ cup sauerkraut mixture)

1 (2-pound) pork tenderloin, trimmed

1 cup chopped onion (about 1 medium)

¾ cup apricot preserves

½ cup dried apricots

½ cup pitted dried plums

¼ cup fat-free, lower-sodium chicken broth

¼ cup orange juice

2 tablespoons cornstarch

1 teaspoon salt

½ teaspoon dried thyme

¼ teaspoon freshly ground black pepper

1 (10-ounce) package refrigerated sauerkraut

1. Place pork in an electric slow cooker. Combine onion and remaining ingredients in a large bowl; pour sauerkraut mixture over pork. Cover and cook on LOW for 7 hours. Remove pork from slow cooker. Let stand 10 minutes. Cut pork into ¼-inch-thick slices. Serve sliced pork with sauerkraut mixture.

CALORIES 261; FAT 2.5g (sat 0.8g, mono 0.9g, poly 0.4g); PROTEIN 24.6g; CARB 34.9g; FIBER 2.3g; CHOL 74mg; IRON 1.5mg; SODIUM 585mg; CALC 21mg

Plum Pork Tenderloin

Serve with jasmine rice to help soak up some of the sauce. Snow peas make a great side dish for rounding out your meal.

Yield: 8 servings (serving size: 3 ounces pork and ½ cup sauce)

1 tablespoon ground cinnamon

1 tablespoon ground allspice

2 (1-pound) pork tenderloins, trimmed

Cooking spray

1 (9.3-ounce) jar plum sauce

½ cup water

2 plums, each cut into 6 wedges

1. Combine cinnamon and allspice; rub over pork. Place pork in a 5-quart electric slow cooker coated with cooking spray. Pour plum sauce over pork; add ½ cup water and plum wedges. Cover and cook on HIGH for 4 hours or until tender. Serve pork with sauce.

CALORIES 199; FAT 2.9g (sat 0.8g, mono 1g, poly 0.6g); PROTEIN 24.3g; CARB 17.6g; FIBER 1.3g; CHOL 74mg; IRON 1.7mg; SODIUM 238mg; CALC 23mg

INGREDIENT TIP

Ripe plums yield slightly to the touch, but don't squeeze them. Let the fruit sit in your palm. It should give a little. If you buy firm fruit, don't put it in the refrigerator or the kitchen window—put it in a paper bag in a dark place for a day or two to ripen.

Curried Pork over Basmati Rice

Madras curry powder lends a little spice without being overpowering. Coconut milk stirred in at the end of the cooking time counters the burn with sweet creaminess. Reminiscent of many Indian-inspired dishes, this recipe relies on slow cooking to develop its richness.

Yield: 6 servings (serving size: about 1 cup pork mixture and ½ cup rice)

1 teaspoon canola oil

1½ pounds boneless pork loin, cut into 1-inch cubes

3½ cups cubed red potato

1 cup chopped onion

1 cup chopped red bell pepper

¼ cup fat-free, lower-sodium chicken broth

2 tablespoons all-purpose flour

1 tablespoon sugar

2 tablespoons tomato paste

1 tablespoon minced peeled fresh ginger

1½ teaspoons salt

1 teaspoon Madras curry powder

1 teaspoon ground cumin

2 garlic cloves, minced

½ cup coconut milk

3 cups hot cooked basmati rice

Cilantro sprigs (optional)

1. Heat a large skillet. Add oil to pan; swirl to coat. Add pork; cook 4 minutes, browning on all sides.

2. Combine potato and next 11 ingredients (through garlic) in an electric slow cooker; stir well to dissolve flour. Cover and cook on LOW for 6 to 8 hours or until pork and potatoes are tender. Stir in coconut milk. Serve pork over rice. Garnish each serving with a cilantro sprig, if desired.

CALORIES 371; FAT 6.2g (sat 2.4g, mono 1.8g, poly 0.5g); PROTEIN 30.6g; CARB 47g; FIBER 3.4g; CHOL 71mg; IRON 2.9mg; SODIUM 682mg; CALC 29mg

Char Siu Pork Roast

Our recipe for *char siu,* the Chinese version of barbecue, transforms pork into a stress-free entrée. Serve with sticky or long-grain white rice and a steamed or stir-fried medley of bell peppers, carrots, snow peas, sliced baby corn, and water chestnuts.

Yield: 8 servings (serving size: 3 ounces beef and ¼ cup sauce)

¼ cup lower-sodium soy sauce

¼ cup hoisin sauce

3 tablespoons ketchup

3 tablespoons honey

2 teaspoons minced garlic

2 teaspoons grated peeled fresh ginger

1 teaspoon dark sesame oil

½ teaspoon five-spice powder

1 (2-pound) boneless pork shoulder (Boston butt), trimmed

½ cup fat-free, lower-sodium chicken broth

1. Combine first 8 ingredients in a small bowl, stirring well with a whisk. Place in a large zip-top plastic bag. Add pork to bag; seal. Marinate in refrigerator at least 2 hours, turning occasionally.
2. Place pork and marinade in an electric slow cooker. Cover and cook on LOW for 8 hours.
3. Remove pork from slow cooker with a slotted spoon; place on a cutting board or work surface. Cover with aluminum foil; keep warm.
4. Add broth to sauce in slow cooker. Cover and cook on LOW for 30 minutes or until sauce thickens. Shred pork with 2 forks; serve with sauce.

CALORIES 227; FAT 9.5g (sat 3.1g, mono 3.9g, poly 1.1g); PROTEIN 21.6g; CARB 12.7g; FIBER 0.4g; CHOL 73mg; IRON 1.7mg; SODIUM 561mg; CALC 30mg

Pork Vindaloo

Seasoned with ginger, garam masala, mustard seeds, and cumin, this fragrant Indian-spiced pork loin braises in a tomato-based sauce. The low-and-slow cooking method renders the pork melt-in-your-mouth tender.

Yield: 6 servings (serving size: 1 cup pork mixture, ½ cup rice, and 1 teaspoon cilantro)

1½ tablespoons minced peeled fresh ginger

2 teaspoons garam masala

2 teaspoons mustard seeds

½ teaspoon salt

1½ teaspoons ground cumin

½ teaspoon ground red pepper

1 (2-pound) boneless pork loin roast, trimmed and cut into 1-inch pieces

2 cups chopped onion

6 garlic cloves, minced

1.1 ounces all-purpose flour (about ¼ cup)

⅓ cup dry red wine

2½ cups coarsely chopped tomato (about 1 pound)

3 cups hot cooked basmati rice

2 tablespoons chopped fresh cilantro

1. Combine first 6 ingredients in a meduim bowl. Add pork, tossing to coat.

2. Heat a large nonstick skillet over medium-high heat. Add pork to pan. Cook 5 minutes or until pork is lightly browned on all sides. Place pork in a 4-quart electric slow cooker.

3. Add onion and garlic to pan; reduce heat to medium, and sauté 5 minutes or until onion is crisp-tender. Stir in flour. Add wine, scraping pan to loosen browned bits. Add tomato to onion mixture. Spoon onion mixture over pork. Cover and cook on LOW for 7 hours or until pork is tender. Serve over rice; sprinkle with cilantro.

CALORIES 379; FAT 7.2g (sat 1.9g, mono 2.5g, poly 0.7g); PROTEIN 38.4g; CARB 36.2g; FIBER 2.7g; CHOL 95mg; IRON 3.1mg; SODIUM 279mg; CALC 43mg

Pork Carnitas

Serve with black beans and rice, if desired.

Yield: 10 servings (serving size: 3 ounces pork, 2 tortillas, 1 tablespoon onion, 1 tablespoon salsa, 1 tablespoon cilantro, and 1 lime wedge)

1 (3-pound) boneless pork shoulder (Boston butt), trimmed

10 garlic cloves, sliced

2 teaspoons ground cumin

1 teaspoon dried oregano

¾ teaspoon salt

½ teaspoon freshly ground black pepper

¾ cup orange juice

2 tablespoons fresh lime juice

2 chipotle chiles canned in adobo sauce, drained and chopped

20 (6-inch) flour or corn tortillas, warmed

⅔ cup chopped onion

⅔ cup bottled salsa

⅔ cup chopped fresh cilantro

10 lime wedges

1. Make ½-inch-deep slits on outside of roast; stuff with garlic. Combine cumin and next 3 ingredients (through black pepper) in a small bowl. Place roast in a 3½-quart electric slow cooker. Sprinkle pork on all sides with spice mixture.

2. Combine juices and chipotle chiles. Pour juice mixture over pork. Cover and cook on LOW for 8 hours or until pork is tender.

3. Remove pork from slow cooker; shred with 2 forks. Skim fat from cooking liquid. Combine shredded pork and ½ cup cooking liquid; toss well.

4. Spoon 1½ ounces pork mixture onto each tortilla; top each with 1½ teaspoons onion, 1½ teaspoons salsa, and 1½ teaspoons cilantro. Serve with lime wedges.

CALORIES 334; FAT 12.6g (sat 3.9g, mono 5.1g, poly 1.7g); PROTEIN 29.4g; CARB 27.1g; FIBER 3g; CHOL 87mg; IRON 2.1mg; SODIUM 424mg; CALC 81mg

Sausage Jambalaya

Round out this meal with a small green salad and a slice of toasted French baguette.

Yield: 8 servings (serving size: about 1 cup jambalaya and ½ cup rice)

2 cups chopped onion

1 cup chopped celery

1 cup water

½ teaspoon Cajun seasoning

½ teaspoon dried thyme

1 pound skinless, boneless chicken thighs, cut into 1-inch cubes

8 ounces andouille sausage, sliced

1 (14.5-ounce) can diced tomatoes and green chiles, undrained

1 pound medium shrimp, peeled and deveined

4 cups hot cooked rice

Chopped green onions (optional)

1. Combine first 8 ingredients in a 4-quart electric slow cooker. Cover and cook on LOW for 6 hours. Stir in shrimp; cover and cook on LOW for 10 minutes or just until shrimp are done. Serve over rice. Sprinkle with green onions, if desired.

CALORIES 315; FAT 8.5g (sat 3g, mono 3.1g, poly 1.4g); PROTEIN 30g; CARB 27.9g; FIBER 1.3g; CHOL 149mg; IRON 3.6mg; SODIUM 404mg; CALC 61mg

QUICK TIP

To cut down on prep time, purchase prechopped onion and celery that you'll find in most grocers' produce departments. They are real time-savers.

Red Beans and Rice

The ultimate in thriftiness and convenience, slow cooking beans and sausage together coaxes all the flavor from the sausage right into the beans. You can also cook this dish on LOW for 8 hours.

Yield: 4 servings (serving size: 1 cup bean mixture, ¾ cup rice, and 1 tablespoon green onions)

3 cups water

1 cup dried red kidney beans

1 cup chopped onion

1 cup chopped green bell pepper

¾ cup chopped celery

1 teaspoon dried thyme

1 teaspoon paprika

¾ teaspoon ground red pepper

½ teaspoon freshly ground black pepper

½ (14-ounce) package turkey, pork, and beef smoked sausage, thinly sliced

1 bay leaf

5 garlic cloves, minced

½ teaspoon salt

3 cups hot cooked long-grain rice

¼ cup chopped green onions

1. Combine first 12 ingredients in an electric slow cooker. Cover and cook on HIGH for 5 hours. Discard bay leaf; stir in salt. Serve over rice; sprinkle servings evenly with green onions.

CALORIES 413; FAT 2.5g (sat 0.7g, mono 0.2g, poly 0.5g); PROTEIN 21.1g; CARB 76.3g; FIBER 10.1g; CHOL 18mg; IRON 6mg; SODIUM 749mg; CALC 102mg

SUBSTITUTION TIP

If you don't have long-grain rice in your pantry, it's perfectly acceptable to substitute brown rice—or even instant rice, if you're in a pinch.

Spiced Apple Pork Chops

Essential to the recipe, the thickness of the pork chops ensures that the chops stay tender and juicy throughout the long cook time. Mashed sweet potatoes and sautéed Brussels sprouts complete the comforting meal.

Yield: 4 servings (serving size: 1 pork chop and ¾ cup apple mixture)

4 (8-ounce) bone-in center-cut pork chops (about 1 inch thick)

¼ teaspoon salt

½ teaspoon freshly ground black pepper

1 teaspoon canola oil

Cooking spray

1 (8-ounce) container refrigerated prechopped onion (about 1¾ cups)

2 cups water

¼ cup firmly packed brown sugar

1 teaspoon ground cinnamon

½ teaspoon ground cloves

½ teaspoon ground ginger

1 (5-ounce) package dried apples

1. Sprinkle pork with salt and pepper. Heat a large nonstick skillet over medium-high heat. Add oil to pan; swirl to coat. Add pork to pan; cook 3 minutes on each side or until browned. Transfer pork to a 5-quart electric slow cooker coated with cooking spray, reserving drippings in pan. Reduce heat to medium. Add onion to drippings in pan; sauté 3 minutes or until tender. Stir in 2 cups water, scraping pan to loosen browned bits. Stir in brown sugar and next 3 ingredients (through ginger). Remove pan from heat.
2. Add apples to slow cooker; pour onion mixture over apples. Cover and cook on LOW for 3 to 3½ hours or until tender. Serve pork chops with apple mixture.

CALORIES 391; FAT 9.7g (sat 2.6g, mono 3.7g, poly 1.3g); PROTEIN 31.7g; CARB 43.8g; FIBER 4.2g; CHOL 94mg; IRON 1.9mg; SODIUM 457mg; CALC 60mg

Caribbean-Style Pork

Yield: 6 servings (serving size: ¾ cup rice, ⅔ cup pork mixture, and 1 teaspoon green onions)

1 (2-pound) boneless center-cut pork loin roast, trimmed

1 teaspoon olive oil

2 cups chopped red bell pepper

6 green onions, cut into 1-inch pieces

Cooking spray

2 tablespoons hoisin sauce

1 tablespoon lower-sodium soy sauce

1 tablespoon fresh lime juice

2 tablespoons creamy peanut butter

1 teaspoon cumin seeds, crushed

½ teaspoon salt

½ teaspoon crushed red pepper

2 garlic cloves, minced

4½ cups hot cooked basmati rice

2 tablespoons diagonally sliced green onions

1. Cut roast into 1-inch pieces. Heat a large nonstick skillet over medium heat. Add oil to pan; swirl to coat. Add pork; sauté 5 minutes or until browned.

2. Place pork, bell pepper, and green onion pieces in a 4-quart electric slow cooker coated with cooking spray; stir well.

3. Combine hoisin sauce and next 7 ingredients (through garlic) in a small bowl; stir until well blended. Pour mixture over pork and vegetables; stir well.

4. Cover and cook on HIGH for 1 hour. Reduce heat to LOW, and cook for 5 to 6 hours. Serve over rice; sprinkle with sliced green onions.

CALORIES 422; FAT 10.6g (sat 2.8g, mono 4.8g, poly 1.6g); PROTEIN 37.4g; CARB 42g; FIBER 2.4g; CHOL 95mg; IRON 3.6mg; SODIUM 547mg; CALC 38mg

FLAVOR TIP

With their crisp texture and sweet flavor, bell peppers are a nice complement to the pork in this dish. If you plan to use the peppers within a day or two, keep them at room temperature for better flavor.

Chinese Pork Tenderloin with Garlic-Sauced Noodles

Yield: 9 servings (serving size: 1⅓ cups noodle mixture, 1 teaspoon peanuts, 2 teaspoons cilantro, and 1 lime wedge)

2 (1-pound) pork tenderloins, trimmed

¼ cup lower-sodium soy sauce, divided

1 tablespoon hoisin sauce

1 tablespoon tomato sauce

1 teaspoon sugar

1 teaspoon grated peeled fresh ginger

2 garlic cloves, minced

3 tablespoons seasoned rice vinegar

1 teaspoon dark sesame oil

8 cups hot cooked Chinese-style noodles (about 16 ounces uncooked)

1 cup matchstick-cut carrots

¾ cup diagonally sliced green onions

¼ cup fresh cilantro leaves

⅓ cup chopped unsalted, dry-roasted peanuts

⅓ cup chopped fresh cilantro

9 lime wedges

1. Place tenderloins in a 5-quart electric slow cooker. Combine 1 tablespoon soy sauce and next 5 ingredients (through garlic); drizzle over tenderloins. Cover and cook on LOW for 3½ hours. Remove pork from slow cooker, and place in a large bowl, reserving cooking liquid in slow cooker. Let pork stand 10 minutes.

2. Strain cooking liquid through a sieve into a bowl. Cover and keep warm. Shred pork with 2 forks.

3. Return cooking liquid to slow cooker; stir in remaining 3 tablespoons soy sauce, vinegar, and sesame oil. Cover and cook on HIGH 10 minutes. Turn slow cooker off. Add pork, noodles, and next 3 ingredients (through cilantro leaves), tossing to coat. Spoon noodle mixture into bowls; sprinkle with peanuts and chopped cilantro. Serve with lime wedges.

CALORIES 303; FAT 5.7g (sat 1.2g, mono 2.3g, poly 1.4g); PROTEIN 28.3g; CARB 34.1g; FIBER 2.7g; CHOL 72mg; IRON 3.1mg; SODIUM 555mg; CALC 30mg

Cabbage Rolls

Yield: 6 servings (serving size: 2 cabbage rolls and about ½ cup sauerkraut mixture)

12 large green cabbage leaves

3 cups chopped onion

½ cup uncooked instant rice

½ pound lean ground pork

½ pound 50%-less-fat pork breakfast sausage

¼ teaspoon freshly ground black pepper

1 (14.4-ounce) can shredded sauerkraut, rinsed and drained

½ teaspoon caraway seeds

Cooking spray

2 cups low-sodium tomato juice

2 tablespoons light brown sugar

3 tablespoons tomato paste

1. Cook cabbage leaves in boiling water 3 to 4 minutes or just until tender. Drain.

2. Heat a large nonstick skillet over medium-high heat. Add onion; sauté 5 to 7 minutes or until tender. Remove pan from heat; stir in rice. Cool 15 minutes.

3. Combine rice mixture, pork, sausage, and pepper. Spoon about ¼ cup mixture into center of 1 cabbage leaf. Fold in edges of leaves. Starting at stem end, roll up jelly-roll fashion. Repeat procedure with remaining leaves and filling.

4. Combine sauerkraut and caraway seeds. Spoon half of sauerkraut mixture into a 4-quart electric slow cooker coated with cooking spray. Top with half of cabbage rolls, seam sides down. Repeat layers with remaining sauerkraut mixture and cabbage rolls.

5. Combine tomato juice, brown sugar, and tomato paste, stirring with a whisk. Pour tomato juice mixture over cabbage rolls. Cover and cook on LOW for 6 hours. Serve rolls with sauerkraut mixture.

CALORIES 287; FAT 10.8g (sat 3.8g, mono 0.1g, poly 0.1g); PROTEIN 17.7g; CARB 31g; FIBER 5.9g; CHOL 55mg; IRON 3mg; SODIUM 780mg; CALC 79mg

Braised Pork Loin with Port and Dried Plums

Yield: 10 servings (serving size: 3 ounces pork and ½ cup sauce)

1 (3¼-pound) boneless pork loin roast, trimmed

1½ teaspoons freshly ground black pepper

1 teaspoon salt

1 teaspoon dry mustard

1 teaspoon dried sage (not rubbed sage)

½ teaspoon dried thyme

1 tablespoon olive oil

2 cups sliced onion

1 cup finely chopped leek

1 cup finely chopped carrot

½ cup port or other sweet red wine

⅓ cup fat-free, lower-sodium chicken broth

⅓ cup water

1 cup pitted dried plums (about 20 dried plums)

2 bay leaves

2 tablespoons cornstarch

2 tablespoons water

1. Cut roast in half crosswise. Combine pepper and next 4 ingredients (through thyme). Rub seasoning mixture over surface of roast halves.

2. Heat a large Dutch oven over medium-high heat. Add oil to pan; swirl to coat. Add pork, browning on all sides. Place pork in a 4½-quart electric slow cooker. Add onion, leek, and carrot to Dutch oven; sauté 5 minutes or until vegetables are golden. Stir in wine, broth, and ⅓ cup water, scraping pan to loosen browned bits. Pour wine mixture over pork in slow cooker; add plums and bay leaves. Cover and cook on HIGH for 1 hour. Reduce heat to LOW, and cook for 5 to 6 hours or until pork is tender.

3. Remove pork from slow cooker; reserve cooking liquid in slow cooker. Set pork aside; keep warm. Increase heat to HIGH. Combine cornstarch and 2 tablespoons water; stir well, and add to cooking liquid. Cook, uncovered, 15 minutes or until mixture is thick, stirring frequently. Discard bay leaves. Slice pork, and serve with sauce.

CALORIES 280; FAT 7.8g (sat 2.4g, mono 3.9g, poly 0.8g); PROTEIN 32.2g; CARB 17.7g; FIBER 2g; CHOL 93mg; IRON 2mg; SODIUM 340mg; CALC 40mg

Rosemary Pork Sliders with Horseradish Aioli

Assemble the sliders before dinner. Or, consider showcasing a slider assembly station for your family or friends to make their own.

Yield: 12 servings (serving size: 2 sliders)

1 (1½-pound) boneless pork loin roast, trimmed

½ teaspoon freshly ground black pepper

Cooking spray

1 cup water

1 cup fat-free, lower-sodium chicken broth

½ cup vertically sliced shallots (2 large)

1 tablespoon chopped fresh rosemary

4 garlic cloves, minced

¾ cup canola mayonnaise

2 teaspoons prepared horseradish

24 (1.3-ounce) wheat slider buns, split and toasted

2 cups arugula

1. Sprinkle pork with pepper. Heat a large skillet over medium-high heat. Add pork; cook 3 minutes on each side or until browned. Transfer pork to a 3-quart slow cooker coated with cooking spray. Add 1 cup water and next 4 ingredients (through garlic) to slow cooker. Cover and cook on LOW for 8 hours or until tender.

2. Remove pork from slow cooker; place in a bowl. Shred pork with 2 forks. Pour cooking liquid through a sieve into a bowl, reserving shallots and garlic. Add ¾ cup strained cooking liquid, shallots, and garlic to pork; toss well. Discard remaining cooking liquid.

3. Combine mayonnaise and horseradish in a small bowl. Spoon about 2 tablespoons pork mixture on bottom half of each bun. Top evenly with arugula. Spread 1½ teaspoons mayonnaise mixture on cut side of each bun top. Cover sliders with bun tops.

CALORIES 421; FAT 20.2g (sat 2.9g, mono 8.3g, poly 3.4g); PROTEIN 26.1g; CARB 35.8g; FIBER 2.2g; CHOL 50mg; IRON 2.9mg; SODIUM 479mg; CALC 105mg

Pork and Slaw Sandwiches

Yield: 15 servings (serving size: 1 sandwich)

1 (3-pound) boneless pork loin roast, trimmed

1 cup water

1¾ cups barbecue sauce

2 tablespoons brown sugar

1½ tablespoons hot sauce

½ teaspoon freshly ground black pepper

2½ cups packaged cabbage-and-carrot coleslaw

¼ cup canola mayonnaise

1 tablespoon white vinegar

¼ teaspoon sugar

⅛ teaspoon salt

15 (2-ounce) hamburger buns

1. Place pork and 1 cup water in a 3- to 4-quart electric slow cooker. Cover and cook on LOW for 7 hours or until meat is tender.

2. Drain pork, discarding cooking liquid. Return pork to slow cooker; shred with 2 forks. Stir in barbecue sauce and next 3 ingredients (through pepper). Cover and cook on LOW for 1 hour.

3. Combine coleslaw and next 4 ingredients (through salt) in a bowl; toss well. Place about ⅓ cup pork mixture and about 2 tablespoons slaw on bottom half of each bun; cover with bun tops.

CALORIES 330; FAT 8.7g (sat 2.1g, mono 3.8g, poly 2.1g); PROTEIN 23.4g; CARB 38.1g; FIBER 1.3g; CHOL 59mg; IRON 2.3mg; SODIUM 565mg; CALC 78mg

QUICK TIP

Using packaged cabbage-and-carrot coleslaw shaves time off the prep. Long gone are the days when you'd have to shred your own.

Stuffed Squash

Serve this classic Middle Eastern meal in bowls so you can scoop up every drop of the tasty sauce with warm pita bread. Offer a salad of chopped lettuce, cucumber, and feta cheese.

Yield: 4 servings (serving size: 2 squash and 1 cup sauce)

8 medium yellow squash (about 3 pounds)

4 teaspoons minced garlic, divided

8 ounces lean ground lamb

¼ cup uncooked converted rice

¼ cup chopped fresh parsley

1 tablespoon chopped fresh mint

¼ teaspoon salt

¾ teaspoon ground allspice

¾ teaspoon ground cinnamon

½ teaspoon freshly ground black pepper

Cooking spray

½ cup finely chopped onion

2 teaspoons brown sugar

1 (15-ounce) can no-salt-added tomato sauce

1 (14.5-ounce) can petite diced tomatoes, undrained

8 teaspoons chopped fresh mint (optional)

1. Cut off narrow neck of each squash. Insert a small paring knife into cut ends of squash. Carefully twist knife to remove pulp. (Do not pierce sides of squash.)

2. Combine 2 teaspoons garlic, lamb, and next 7 ingredients (through pepper) in a bowl. Stuff lamb mixture evenly into squash to within ¼ inch of opening. Place squash horizontally, slightly overlapping, in a 5-quart electric slow cooker coated with cooking spray.

3. Combine remaining 2 teaspoons garlic, onion, and next 3 ingredients (through tomatoes); pour over squash. Cover and cook on LOW for 6 hours or until squash is tender and filling is done. Serve squash with sauce; sprinkle with additional mint, if desired.

CALORIES 347; FAT 14.7g (sat 5.9g, mono 5.5g, poly 1.4g); PROTEIN 15.8g; CARB 38.4g; FIBER 5.7g; CHOL 41mg; IRON 3.5mg; SODIUM 507mg; CALC 137mg

Apricot Lamb Tagine

Serve this filling Moroccan-style lamb stew over hot couscous with a side of steamed green beans.

Yield: 8 servings (serving size: ½ cup couscous, ½ cup lamb mixture, 1½ teaspoons almonds, and 1½ teaspoons parsley)

Tagine:

2 cups diced onion (about 1 large)

½ cup orange juice

½ cup lower-sodium beef broth

1 tablespoon grated lemon rind

2 tablespoons honey

1 tablespoon fresh lemon juice

2 teaspoons minced garlic

2 teaspoons grated peeled fresh ginger

1½ teaspoons salt

1 teaspoon ground coriander

½ teaspoon ground cumin

¼ teaspoon freshly ground black pepper

2 pounds boneless leg of lamb, trimmed and cut into bite-sized pieces

2 (3-inch) cinnamon sticks

1 (6-ounce) package dried apricots, halved

Remaining ingredients:

4 cups hot cooked couscous

¼ cup slivered almonds, toasted

¼ cup chopped fresh parsley

1. To prepare tagine, combine first 15 ingredients in an electric slow cooker. Cover and cook on LOW for 8 hours. Discard cinnamon sticks.

2. Place couscous on each of 8 plates. Top each serving with lamb mixture, almonds, and parsley.

CALORIES 451; FAT 18.7g (sat 7.1g, mono 8.1g, poly 1.7g); PROTEIN 26.2g; CARB 43.2g; FIBER 3.6g; CHOL 81mg; IRON 3.3mg; SODIUM 515mg; CALC 52mg

Lamb Tagine

The intriguing combination of lamb, saffron, sweet spices, and dried plums makes this slow-cooker meal suitable for supper club and easy entertaining.

Yield: 6 servings (serving size: ½ cup couscous, ⅔ cup lamb mixture, and 1 teaspoon almonds)

1 navel orange

2 tablespoons all-purpose flour

2 pounds boneless leg of lamb, trimmed and cut into 1½-inch cubes

½ cup fat-free, lower-sodium chicken broth

2 cups chopped white onion

1 teaspoon pumpkin pie spice

1 teaspoon ground cumin

½ teaspoon salt

¼ teaspoon saffron threads, crushed

¼ teaspoon ground red pepper

1 cup pitted dried plums

2 tablespoons honey

3 cups hot cooked couscous

2 tablespoons slivered almonds, toasted

1. Grate rind and squeeze juice from orange to measure 2 teaspoons and ¼ cup, respectively. Add flour to orange juice, stirring with a whisk until smooth; stir in rind.

2. Heat a large nonstick skillet over medium-high heat. Add lamb; sauté 7 minutes or until browned. Stir in broth, scraping pan to loosen brown bits. Stir in orange juice mixture. Stir onion and next 5 ingredients (through red pepper) into lamb mixture. Pour mixture into a 3-quart electric slow cooker. Cover and cook on LOW for 6 hours or until lamb is tender.

3. Stir dried plums and honey into lamb mixture. Cover and cook on LOW for 1 hour or until thoroughly heated. Serve lamb mixture over couscous; sprinkle with almonds.

CALORIES 487; FAT 18.9g (sat 7.5g, mono 7.8g, poly 1.8g); PROTEIN 33.8g; CARB 45.1g; FIBER 4.1g; CHOL 101mg; IRON 3.6mg; SODIUM 332mg; CALC 53mg

Zinfandel-Braised Leg of Lamb

Reducing the wine before placing it in the slow cooker gives the dish a more complex flavor.

Yield: 6 servings (serving size: 3 ounces lamb, ¼ cup cooking liquid, and 1 cup noodles)

1 (2½-pound) rolled boneless leg of lamb

1 teaspoon kosher salt, divided

1 teaspoon freshly ground black pepper, divided

1 tablespoon all-purpose flour

2 teaspoons olive oil

1 tablespoon juniper berries, crushed

1 teaspoon whole allspice, crushed

6 garlic cloves, sliced

1 cup zinfandel or other fruity dry red wine

1 teaspoon dried basil

2 bay leaves

6 cups hot cooked egg noodles (about 4¾ cups uncooked pasta)

1. Unroll lamb; trim fat. Sprinkle evenly with ½ teaspoon salt and ½ teaspoon pepper. Reroll lamb; secure at 1-inch intervals with twine. Sprinkle evenly with flour. Heat a skillet over medium-high heat. Add oil to pan; swirl to coat. Add lamb to pan; cook 6 minutes, browning on all sides. Place lamb in an electric slow cooker. Add juniper berries, allspice, and garlic to pan; cook over medium heat 2 minutes or until garlic is lightly browned. Add wine to pan, scraping pan to loosen browned bits; cook until reduced to ½ cup (about 3 minutes). Scrape wine mixture into slow cooker; add basil and bay leaves. Cover and cook on LOW for 8 hours or until lamb is tender.

2. Remove lamb from slow cooker; keep warm. Strain cooking liquid through a sieve into a bowl; discard solids. Add remaining ½ teaspoon salt and remaining ½ teaspoon pepper to cooking liquid; stir. Remove twine from lamb, and discard. Break lamb into chunks with 2 forks. Serve lamb and cooking liquid over egg noodles.

CALORIES 481; FAT 14.3g (sat 4.2g, mono 6.2g, poly 1.7g); PROTEIN 42.2g; CARB 43.4g; FIBER 2.4g; CHOL 155mg; IRON 5.4mg; SODIUM 408mg; CALC 46mg

Braised Lamb with Picholine Olives

Browning the lamb before it slow cooks in liquid gives this Moroccan-inspired dish added depth of flavor. Serve the tagine over couscous. Preserved lemons add a wonderful citrus piquancy to this dish.

Yield: 8 servings (serving size: ¾ cup lamb mixture and ½ cup couscous)

3 pounds lamb shoulder, trimmed and cut into 1½-inch cubes

1 tablespoon ground coriander

1 large red onion, vertically sliced

1 (14.5-ounce) can diced tomatoes, undrained

½ cup picholine olives, pitted

4 cups hot cooked couscous

1 preserved lemon, halved lengthwise and thinly sliced (optional)

Chopped fresh cilantro (optional)

1. Heat a large nonstick skillet over medium-high heat. Add half of lamb to pan. Cook 5 minutes or until browned, stirring occasionally. Place lamb in a 5-quart electric slow cooker. Repeat procedure with remaining lamb.

2. Add coriander, onion, and tomatoes to slow cooker. Cover and cook on LOW for 7 hours.

3. Add olives. Turn off slow cooker; let stand, covered, 30 minutes.

4. Place couscous in shallow bowls. Spoon lamb mixture over couscous. Garnish with preserved lemon and cilantro, if desired.

CALORIES 354; FAT 11.2g (sat 3.2g, mono 4.1g, poly 0.9g); PROTEIN 37.6g; CARB 21.7g; FIBER 1.3g; CHOL 109mg; IRON 3.3mg; SODIUM 616mg; CALC 56mg

INGREDIENT TIP

Preserved lemons are lemons that have been pickled in salt; their juices appear often in Middle Eastern and Mediterranean cuisines. You can purchase them at specialty markets.

Indian Lamb Curry

A combo of tomato juice and flour creates a thick sauce. Serve with a piece of naan to sop up any extra.

Yield: 8 servings (serving size: ½ cup rice, ⅔ cup lamb curry, 1 tablespoon yogurt, and 1 tablespoon cilantro)

2 pounds boneless leg of lamb, trimmed and cut into 1-inch cubes

1 (14.5-ounce) can diced tomatoes, undrained

2 tablespoons all-purpose flour

2 cups finely chopped white onion

2 tablespoons grated peeled fresh ginger

2 teaspoons mustard seeds

2 teaspoons garam masala

2 teaspoons ground cumin

½ teaspoon salt

¼ teaspoon ground red pepper

4 garlic cloves, minced

4 cups hot cooked basmati rice

½ cup plain fat-free yogurt

½ cup chopped fresh cilantro

1. Heat a large nonstick skillet over medium-high heat. Add lamb; sauté 5 minutes or until browned. Remove lamb from pan; place in a 4-quart electric slow cooker.

2. Drain tomatoes, reserving juice. Place flour in a small bowl; gradually add tomato juice, stirring with a whisk until smooth. Stir tomatoes, tomato juice mixture, onion, and next 7 ingredients (through garlic) into lamb. Cover and cook on LOW for 8 hours or until lamb is tender. Serve lamb curry over rice; top with yogurt, and sprinkle with cilantro.

CALORIES 302; FAT 6.4g (sat 2.1g, mono 2.3g, poly 0.6g); PROTEIN 27.5g; CARB 32g; FIBER 1.4g; CHOL 75mg; IRON 3.8mg; SODIUM 372mg; CALC 72mg

Tarragon Lamb Shanks with Cannellini Beans

Yield: 12 servings (serving size: about 3 ounces lamb and ⅔ cup bean mixture)

4 (1½-pound) lamb shanks

1 (19-ounce) can cannellini beans or other white beans, rinsed and drained

1½ cups diced peeled carrot

1 cup chopped onion

¾ cup chopped celery

2 garlic cloves, thinly sliced

2 teaspoons dried tarragon

½ teaspoon salt

¼ teaspoon freshly ground black pepper

1 (28-ounce) can diced tomatoes, undrained

1. Trim fat from lamb shanks. Place beans and next 4 ingredients (through garlic) in a 7-quart electric slow cooker; stir well. Place lamb shanks on bean mixture; sprinkle with tarragon, salt, and pepper. Pour tomatoes over lamb. Cover and cook on HIGH for 1 hour. Reduce heat to LOW, and cook 9 hours or until lamb is very tender.

2. Remove lamb shanks from slow cooker. Pour bean mixture through a colander or sieve over a bowl, reserving liquid. Let liquid stand 5 minutes; skim fat from surface of liquid. Return bean mixture to liquid. Remove lamb from bones; discard bones. Serve lamb with bean mixture.

CALORIES 353; FAT 10.3g (sat 3.7g, mono 4.1g, poly 1g); PROTEIN 50.3g; CARB 12.9g; FIBER 2.9g; CHOL 145mg; IRON 4.9mg; SODIUM 554mg; CALC 80mg

NUTRITION TIP

Canned beans are a convenient option when you don't have time to prepare dried beans—the drawback is the

sodium content. Reduce the sodium content of any variety of canned beans by 40 percent simply by draining and rinsing them.

Meatballs with Chutney Sauce

To ensure that you get a lean product, ask the butcher to grind a lean boneless leg of lamb.

Yield: 6 servings (serving size: 6 meatballs, 2½ tablespoons sauce, ½ cup couscous, and ½ teaspoon mint)

1 (1-ounce) slice white bread, torn into pieces

1½ pounds lean ground lamb

¼ cup finely chopped green onions

2 tablespoons minced seeded pickled jalapeño peppers

½ teaspoon freshly ground black pepper

2 garlic cloves, minced

1 large egg

½ cup mango chutney

¼ cup no-salt-added tomato paste

3 tablespoons lower-sodium soy sauce

1 tablespoon pickled jalapeño pepper liquid

2 teaspoons finely chopped fresh mint

3 cups hot cooked couscous

1 tablespoon thinly sliced fresh mint

1. Place bread in a food processor; pulse 2 times or until coarse crumbs measure ½ cup. Combine breadcrumbs, lamb, and next 5 ingredients (through egg) in a bowl. Shape into 36 (1¼-inch) meatballs.

2. Heat a large nonstick skillet over medium-high heat. Add one-third of meatballs; cook 1 minute, shaking pan to brown on all sides. Transfer meatballs to a 3½-or 4-quart slow cooker. Repeat procedure twice with remaining meatballs.

3. Combine chutney and next 4 ingredients (through chopped mint) in a bowl; pour over meatballs. Cover and cook on LOW for 2 hours. Serve meatballs and sauce over couscous. Sprinkle with thinly sliced mint.

CALORIES 387; FAT 7.4g (sat 2.5g, mono 2.8g, poly 0.9g); PROTEIN 29.6g; CARB 47g; FIBER 2.3g; CHOL 110mg; IRON 3.5mg; SODIUM 655mg; CALC 47mg

Osso Buco with Gremolata

Inexpensive veal shanks become a succulent meal in the slow cooker. Even if you aren't an anchovy lover, don't omit the anchovy paste—it adds immeasurably to the flavor. Use the remaining broth mixture in soups and stews.

Yield: 8 servings (serving size: 1 cup pasta, ⅔ cup veal, ½ cup broth mixture, and 1 tablespoon gremolata)

Osso buco:

3 ounces all-purpose flour (about ⅔ cup)

¾ teaspoon freshly ground black pepper, divided

½ teaspoon kosher salt, divided

6 veal shanks, trimmed (about 5 pounds)

2 teaspoons butter, divided

2 teaspoons olive oil, divided

2 cups coarsely chopped red onion

1½ cups chopped celery

6 garlic cloves, minced

4 cups beef broth

2 cups dry white wine

1 tablespoon chopped fresh rosemary

1 tablespoon anchovy paste

Gremolata:

½ cup chopped fresh flat-leaf parsley

1 tablespoon grated lemon rind

2 garlic cloves, minced

Remaining ingredient:

8 cups hot cooked pappardelle (about 1 pound uncooked wide ribbon pasta)

1. To prepare osso buco, combine flour, ¼ teaspoon pepper, and ¼ teaspoon salt in a shallow dish. Dredge veal in flour mixture.

2. Heat a large skillet over medium heat. Add 1 teaspoon butter and 1 teaspoon oil; cook until butter melts. Add half of veal; cook 6 minutes, browning on both sides. Place browned veal in a large electric slow cooker. Repeat procedure with remaining butter, oil, and veal.

3. Add onion and celery to pan; sauté 5 minutes over medium-high heat or until tender. Add 6 garlic cloves to pan; sauté 1 minute. Stir in broth, wine, rosemary, and anchovy paste, scraping pan to loosen browned bits. Bring to a boil; cook 4 minutes. Pour over veal.

4. Cover and cook on LOW for 9 hours or until done. Sprinkle veal with remaining ½ teaspoon pepper and remaining ¼ teaspoon salt. Remove veal from slow cooker; cool slightly.

5. To prepare gremolata, combine parsley, lemon rind, and 2 garlic cloves. Place pasta in each of 8 pasta bowls. Top each serving with veal and broth mixture. (Reserve remaining broth mixture for another use.) Sprinkle each serving with gremolata.

CALORIES 443; FAT 12.2g (sat 4.1g, mono 4.9g, poly 1.1g); PROTEIN 54.9g; CARB 15.9g; FIBER 1.8g; CHOL 200mg; IRON 3.3mg; SODIUM 485mg; CALC 94mg

Ragout of Veal

Yield: 8 servings (serving size: 1 cup pasta, 1 cup ragout, and ¾ teaspoon parsley)

1 (2½-pound) boneless veal tip round roast, trimmed

1½ teaspoons paprika

¾ teaspoon freshly ground black pepper

½ teaspoon salt

1 tablespoon olive oil, divided

½ cup dry white wine

3 cups sliced leek (about 3 large)

3 garlic cloves, minced

1.5 ounces all-purpose flour (about ⅓ cup)

1 (14½-ounce) can chicken broth

3 cups (½-inch) slices peeled carrot

5 thyme sprigs

1 bay leaf

8 cups hot cooked fettuccine (about 16 ounces uncooked pasta

2 tablespoons chopped fresh flat-leaf parsley

1. Cut veal into 1-inch cubes. Sprinkle paprika, pepper, and salt over veal.

2. Heat a large nonstick skillet over medium-high heat. Add 1 teaspoon oil to pan; swirl to coat. Add half of veal; sauté 4 minutes or until browned. Place browned veal in a 6-quart electric slow cooker. Repeat procedure with 1 teaspoon oil and remaining veal. Add wine to skillet; cook 1 minute, scraping pan to loosen browned bits. Pour over veal in slow cooker.

3. Heat skillet over medium-high heat. Add remaining 1 teaspoon oil to pan; swirl to coat. Add leek and garlic; sauté 3 minutes. Spoon leek mixture over veal in slow cooker.

4. Place flour in a small bowl; gradually add broth, stirring until well blended. Pour broth mixture into slow cooker. Add carrot, thyme sprigs, and bay leaf; stir well. Cover and cook on LOW for 3 to 5 hours or until veal is tender. Discard thyme sprigs and bay leaf. Serve veal mixture over pasta; sprinkle with parsley.

CALORIES 451; FAT 5.4g (sat 1.3g, mono 2.1g, poly 0.9g); PROTEIN 40.2g; CARB 56.6g; FIBER 4.8g; CHOL 111mg; IRON 4.2mg; SODIUM 407mg; CALC 58mg

Veal Paprikash

Yield: 7 servings (serving size: ¾ cup veal mixture, ¾ cup noodles, ½ teaspoon parsley, and 1 teaspoon chives)

1 (2¼-pound) lean boneless veal tip round roast, trimmed and cut into 1-inch cubes

1 (8-ounce) package presliced fresh mushrooms

1½ cups sliced carrot

1 cup slivered onion

2 tablespoons chopped fresh parsley

4 garlic cloves, minced

2 bay leaves

2.25 ounces all-purpose flour (about ½ cup)

1 tablespoon Hungarian sweet paprika

¾ teaspoon salt

½ teaspoon dried thyme

½ teaspoon freshly ground black pepper

¼ cup dry white wine

½ cup reduced-fat sour cream

5¼ cups hot cooked medium egg noodles (about 10 ounces uncooked pasta)

3½ teaspoons chopped fresh parsley

7 teaspoons chopped fresh chives

1. Place first 7 ingredients in a 3½-quart electric slow cooker; toss well. Combine flour and next 4 ingredients (through pepper) in a small bowl; gradually add wine, stirring until well blended. Add flour mixture to slow cooker; stir well. Cover and cook on LOW for 6 hours or until veal and vegetables are tender. Discard bay leaves.

2. Turn slow cooker off, and let mixture stand 5 minutes. Stir in sour cream. Serve veal mixture over egg noodles; sprinkle with parsley and chives.

CALORIES 410; FAT 7.2g (sat 2.9g, mono 1.9g, poly 1g); PROTEIN 40.3g; CARB 43.7g; FIBER 3.3g; CHOL 170mg; IRON 3.4mg; SODIUM 390mg; CALC 75mg

INGREDIENT TIP

When storing a bunch of fresh herbs, such as chives or parsley, wrap the stems in a damp paper towel, and store them in a  *zip-top plastic bag in the refrigerator. Wash herbs just before using; pat them dry with a paper towel.*

poultry

Sweet and Sour Chicken

Substitute pork tenderloin in place of chicken thighs, if desired.

Yield: 6 servings (serving size: ⅔ cup chicken mixture and ½ cup rice)

1 cup chopped onion (about 1 medium)

⅓ cup sugar

⅓ cup ketchup

¼ cup orange juice

3 tablespoons cornstarch

3 tablespoons cider vinegar

2 tablespoons lower-sodium soy sauce

1 tablespoon grated peeled fresh ginger

1 pound skinless, boneless chicken thighs, cut into 1-inch pieces

2 (8-ounce) cans pineapple chunks in juice, drained

1 large green bell pepper, cut into ¾-inch pieces

1 large red bell pepper, cut into ¾-inch pieces

3 cups hot cooked white rice

1. Combine first 12 ingredients in an electric slow cooker. Cover and cook on LOW for 6 hours or HIGH for 4 hours. Serve over rice.

CALORIES 332; FAT 3.4g (sat 0.9g, mono 1g, poly 0.9g); PROTEIN 18.4g; CARB 57g; FIBER 1.8g; CHOL 63mg; IRON 2.3mg; SODIUM 348mg; CALC 38mg

EQUIPMENT TIP

To grate ginger quickly, we recommend using a Microplane grater. It's a kitchen must-have.

Tiny French Beans with Smoked Sausage

Find flageolets, tiny French kidney beans, in specialty food stores or online at www.indianharvest.com. For a nice presentation, garnish with thyme sprigs.

Yield: 8 servings (serving size: 1¼ cups)

1 pound smoked turkey sausage, cut into 1½-inch pieces

1 tablespoon canola oil

⅓ cup minced shallots

3 garlic cloves, minced

2 cups dried flageolets or other dried white beans (about 1 pound)

2 cups water

¼ cup minced fresh or 1 tablespoon dried thyme

1 teaspoon celery seeds

¼ teaspoon freshly ground black pepper

1 (14½-ounce) can fat-free, lower-sodium chicken broth

Thyme sprigs (optional)

1. Heat a large nonstick skillet over medium heat. Add sausage; sauté 5 minutes or until browned. Remove from pan, and place in an electric slow cooker. Heat pan over medium heat. Add oil to pan; swirl to coat. Add shallots and garlic; cook 1 minute, stirring constantly.

2. Sort and wash beans. Add beans, shallot mixture, 2 cups water, and next 4 ingredients through broth to slow cooker. Cover and cook on HIGH for 6 hours or until beans are tender. Garnish with thyme sprigs, if desired.

CALORIES 238; FAT 6.2g (sat 1.7g, mono 2.1g, poly 1.8g); PROTEIN 18.9g; CARB 28g; FIBER 8.2g; CHOL 37mg; IRON 3.6mg; SODIUM 689mg; CALC 108mg

Turkey Thighs with Olives and Dried Cherries

Turkey thighs are easy to find, but you also can use a cut-up chicken, if you prefer. This dish is great served with couscous.

Yield: 8 servings (serving size: 3 ounces turkey and about ⅓ cup cooking liquid)

1 cup thinly sliced leek (about 1 large)

1 cup ruby port or other sweet red wine

¾ cup dried cherries

¾ cup pitted kalamata olives

⅓ cup fresh orange juice (about 1 orange)

1 teaspoon paprika

1 teaspoon crushed red pepper

4 thyme sprigs

1 (3-inch) cinnamon stick

3½ pounds turkey thighs, skinned

¼ teaspoon salt

1 tablespoon ground cumin

1. Combine first 9 ingredients in an electric slow cooker, stirring well.
2. Rinse turkey with cold water; pat dry. Sprinkle with salt and cumin. Place in slow cooker. Cover and cook on LOW for 6 hours. Discard thyme sprigs and cinnamon stick. Serve turkey with cooking liquid.

CALORIES 335; FAT 10.5g (sat 2.4g, mono 4.9g, poly 2.2g); PROTEIN 29g; CARB 17.8g; FIBER 2.8g; CHOL 121mg; IRON 5mg; SODIUM 388mg; CALC 56mg

NUTRITION TIP

Turkey skin contains plenty of fat; removing it reduces the fat by about one-third. The skin is easy to remove from thighs.

Mediterranean Roast Turkey

Serve this slow-cooker roast with mashed potatoes and garnish with fresh thyme sprigs, if desired.

Yield: 8 servings (serving size: about 4 ounces turkey and about ⅓ cup onion mixture)

2 cups chopped onion (about 1 large)

½ cup pitted kalamata olives

½ cup julienne-cut drained oil-packed sun-dried tomato halves

2 tablespoons fresh lemon juice

1½ teaspoons minced garlic

1 teaspoon Greek seasoning mix

½ teaspoon salt

¼ teaspoon freshly ground black pepper

1 (4-pound) boneless turkey breast, trimmed

½ cup fat-free, lower-sodium chicken broth, divided

3 tablespoons all-purpose flour

Thyme sprigs (optional)

1. Combine first 9 ingredients in an electric slow cooker. Add ¼ cup chicken broth. Cover and cook on LOW for 7 hours.

2. Combine remaining ¼ cup broth and flour in a small bowl; stir with a whisk until smooth. Add broth mixture to slow cooker. Cover and cook on LOW for 30 minutes. Cut turkey into slices. Serve with onion mixture. Garnish with thyme sprigs, if desired.

CALORIES 314; FAT 4.9g (sat 0.9g, mono 2.6g, poly 0.8g); PROTEIN 57g; CARB 7g; FIBER 0.9g; CHOL 141mg; IRON 3.1mg; SODIUM 468mg; CALC 34mg

Orange-Rosemary Chicken

While this recipe cooks, the aroma of oranges will make your mouth water. The chicken comes out supermoist and juicy.

Yield: 4 servings (serving size: 1 chicken breast half, or 1 chicken thigh and 1 chicken drumstick)

1 large orange

2 tablespoons butter, softened

2 teaspoons chopped fresh rosemary

½ teaspoon kosher salt

½ teaspoon freshly ground black pepper

2 garlic cloves, minced

1 (3½-pound) roasting chicken

Cooking spray

1. Grate rind from half of orange to measure 2 teaspoons. Cut orange half into quarters. Combine orange rind, butter, and next 4 ingredients (through garlic) in a small bowl. (Reserve remaining orange half for another use.)

2. Remove and discard giblets and neck from chicken. Trim excess fat. Starting at neck cavity, loosen skin from breast and drumsticks by inserting fingers, gently pushing between skin and meat. Rub half of butter mixture under loosened skin. Rub remaining butter mixture over surface of chicken. Lift wing tips up and over back; tuck under chicken. Place orange pieces in cavity.

3. Place chicken, breast side up, on a small rack coated with cooking spray. Place rack inside a 5-quart electric slow cooker.

4. Cover and cook on LOW for 4 hours or until a thermometer inserted into meaty part of thigh registers 165°.

5. Remove chicken from slow cooker. Let stand 15 minutes. Discard skin.

CALORIES 296; FAT 11.3g (sat 5g, mono 3.2g, poly 1.6g); PROTEIN 41.7g; CARB 5.1g; FIBER 0.9g; CHOL 147mg; IRON 2.2mg; SODIUM 433mg; CALC 42mg

Chicken Korma

If you prefer milder foods, reduce or omit the crushed red pepper. Add warm naan on the side of this classic Indian dish.

Yield: 8 servings (serving size: about 1 cup chicken mixture, ½ cup rice, and 1½ teaspoons cilantro)

2 pounds skinless, boneless chicken thighs, cut into bite-sized pieces

2 cups coarsely chopped onion (1 onion)

2 tablespoons minced peeled fresh ginger

2 teaspoons curry powder

1 teaspoon ground coriander

½ teaspoon ground cumin

½ teaspoon crushed red pepper

4 garlic cloves, minced

2 cups (½-inch) cubed peeled baking potato

1 teaspoon salt

1 (14.5-ounce) can petite diced tomatoes, undrained

2 bay leaves

1 (3-inch) cinnamon stick

½ cup plain fat-free yogurt

4 cups hot cooked long-grain brown rice

¼ cup chopped fresh cilantro

1. Heat a large nonstick skillet over medium-high heat. Add chicken; sauté 8 minutes or until lightly browned. Remove chicken from pan; place in a 5-quart electric slow cooker. Add onion to pan; sauté 3 minutes. Add ginger and next 5 ingredients (through garlic); sauté 2 minutes. Pour mixture over chicken in slow cooker. Stir in potato and next 4 ingredients (through cinnamon stick).

2. Cover and cook on LOW for 6 hours. Discard bay leaves and cinnamon stick. Turn slow cooker off; let stand 15 minutes. Stir in yogurt. Serve chicken mixture over rice. Sprinkle with cilantro.

CALORIES 297; FAT 5.6g (sat 1.4g, mono 1.7g, poly 1.5g); PROTEIN 26.7g; CARB 34.1g; FIBER 3.7g; CHOL 94mg; IRON 4.1mg; SODIUM 507mg; CALC 63mg

Garlic Chicken

The garlic becomes creamy and mellows as it cooks. Spread it on chunks of crusty French baguette and soak up the fabulous sauce as you enjoy every morsel of this super-tender chicken. If you're tight on time, substitute 3 pounds of chicken pieces rather than cut up the whole chicken. Also, look for garlic cloves that are already peeled.

Yield: 5 servings (serving size: 4 ounces chicken, about 3 tablespoons sauce, and about 8 garlic cloves)

½ cup fat-free, lower-sodium chicken broth

3 tablespoons dry white wine

2 tablespoons cognac

1 (3⅓-pound) whole chicken, skinned and cut into 8 pieces

1½ teaspoons extra-virgin olive oil

1½ teaspoons butter

¼ teaspoon salt

⅛ teaspoon freshly ground black pepper

40 garlic cloves, peeled (about 4 whole heads)

2 teaspoons fresh thyme leaves

4 teaspoons chopped fresh parsley (optional)

1. Combine first 3 ingredients in a small bowl.

2. Discard giblets and neck from chicken. Rinse chicken and pat dry. Heat oil and butter in a 12-inch nonstick skillet over medium-high heat until butter melts. Sprinkle chicken pieces evenly with salt and pepper. Add chicken pieces to pan; cook 2½ minutes on each side or until golden. Remove chicken from pan; place in a 4-quart electric slow cooker.

3. Reduce heat to medium. Add garlic to drippings in pan; sauté 1 minute or until garlic begins to brown. Stir in broth mixture, scraping pan to loosen browned bits. Boil 2 minutes or until sauce is reduced to about 1 cup. Pour sauce over chicken; sprinkle with thyme. Cover and cook on LOW for 4 hours or until chicken is done. Serve sauce and garlic with chicken. Garnish with chopped parsley, if desired.

CALORIES 254; FAT 7.1g (sat 2.1g, mono 2.7g, poly 1.3g); PROTEIN 32.9g; CARB 8.3g; FIBER 0.6g; CHOL 105mg; IRON 1.7mg; SODIUM 297mg; CALC 63mg

Chilaquiles

Before there were nachos, there were chilaquiles. Tomatoes and spices simmer with any kind of meat to make the ideal topping for tortilla chips. Here, chipotle, chicken, and cilantro meld in this filling Mexican favorite.

Yield: 10 servings (serving size: 1½ cups soup, ½ cup tortilla chips, and 1 tablespoon cheese)

4 bone-in chicken breast halves (about 2½ pounds), skinned

1½ cups chopped red onion

1¼ cups chopped red bell pepper

1¼ cups chopped green bell pepper

¾ cup fat-free, lower-sodium chicken broth

¼ cup chopped fresh cilantro

1 tablespoon ground cumin

2 tablespoons chopped chipotle chile, canned in adobo sauce

6 garlic cloves

2 (28-ounce) cans diced fire-roasted tomatoes, undrained

1 (4-ounce) can chopped green chiles, undrained

5 cups baked tortilla chips

2.67 ounces crumbled queso fresco (about ⅔ cup)

1. Heat a large skillet over medium-high heat. Add chicken to pan. Cook 3 minutes on each side or until browned.

2. While chicken cooks, combine onion and next 9 ingredients (through green chiles) in a 5-quart electric slow cooker. Transfer chicken to slow cooker. Cover and cook on LOW for 4 hours.

3. Remove chicken from slow cooker. Remove meat from bones; discard bones. Return meat to soup. Divide tortilla chips among 8 bowls. Ladle soup over tortilla chips; sprinkle with cheese.

CALORIES 219; FAT 2.5g (sat 0.8g, mono 0.6g, poly 0.5g); PROTEIN 25.4g; CARB 22.9g; FIBER 3.8g; CHOL 55mg; IRON 2.3mg; SODIUM 623mg; CALC 92mg

Mediterranean Chicken

Capturing the simplicity found in sun-drenched Mediterranean cuisine, these braised chicken thighs melt under the influence of bright, vibrant lemon, briny olives and capers, and juicy plum tomatoes. Serve with rosemary mashed potatoes or over hot basmati rice.

Yield: 6 servings (serving size: 2 chicken thighs and ½ cup sauce)

1 small lemon

1¾ cups coarsely chopped onion

¼ cup pitted kalamata olives, halved (12 olives)

2 tablespoons drained capers

1 (14.5-ounce) can whole plum tomatoes, drained and coarsely chopped

12 bone-in chicken thighs (about 3 pounds), skinned

¼ teaspoon freshly ground black pepper

1 tablespoon olive oil

Chopped fresh rosemary (optional)

Chopped fresh parsley (optional)

1. Grate rind and squeeze juice from lemon to measure 1 teaspoon and 1 tablespoon, respectively. Place lemon rind in a small bowl. Cover and refrigerate. Combine lemon juice, onion, and next 3 ingredients (through tomatoes) in a 5-quart electric slow cooker.
2. Sprinkle chicken with pepper. Heat a large nonstick skillet over medium-high heat. Add oil to pan; swirl to coat. Place half of chicken in pan; cook 3 minutes on each side or until browned. Place chicken in slow cooker. Repeat procedure with remaining chicken. Cover and cook on LOW for 4 hours or until chicken is done.
3. Place chicken thighs on plates. Stir reserved lemon rind into sauce. Serve sauce over chicken. Garnish with rosemary and parsley, if desired.

CALORIES 220; FAT 8.9g (sat 1.8g, mono 4.4g, poly 1.7g); PROTEIN 26.5g; CARB 7.2g; FIBER 1.4g; CHOL 107mg; IRON 1.8mg; SODIUM 387mg; CALC 35mg

FLAVOR TIP

Piquant, sharp, and tangy are just a few words to describe capers. Use capers  *sparingly to infuse sauces, salads, pizzas, dressings, and pasta or vegetable dishes with flavor.*

Sweet and Spicy Satsuma Turkey

Fresh mandarin oranges, riesling, and orange marmalade provide the highlights for the sweet profile, while crushed red pepper adds the spicy kick to this Asian-inspired turkey dish. Serve with hot steamed rice as an accompaniment to soak up the delicious sauce.

Yield: 8 servings (serving size: 5 ounces turkey and ½ cup sauce)

3 cups thinly sliced red onion (1 large onion)

¾ cup riesling or other slightly sweet white wine

⅔ cup fresh orange juice (2 large oranges)

⅓ cup orange marmalade

2 teaspoons tamarind paste

½ teaspoon crushed red pepper

3¾ pounds bone-in turkey thighs, skinned

2 teaspoons five-spice powder

1 teaspoon salt

1 tablespoon canola oil

2 cups fresh Satsuma mandarin orange sections (about 7 oranges)

1½ tablespoons cornstarch

Sliced green onions (optional)

1. Combine first 6 ingredients in a 5-quart oval electric slow cooker.

2. Rinse turkey with cold water; pat dry. Sprinkle turkey with five-spice powder and salt. Heat a large nonstick skillet over medium-high heat. Add oil to pan; swirl to coat. Add turkey; cook 3 to 4 minutes on each side or until browned. Place turkey in a single layer over onion mixture in slow cooker, overlapping slightly. Add orange sections. Cover and cook on LOW for 4 hours.

3. Remove turkey from slow cooker. Remove bones from turkey; discard bones. Place turkey on a platter. Pour cooking liquid and orange sections into a medium saucepan, reserving ¼ cup cooking liquid. Combine reserved cooking liquid and cornstarch in a small bowl, stirring with a whisk until smooth. Stir cornstarch mixture into orange mixture in saucepan. Bring to a boil; cook, stirring constantly, 1 minute or until sauce thickens.

4. Serve sauce over turkey. Sprinkle with green onions, if desired.

CALORIES 277; FAT 5.7g (sat 1.4g, mono 2g, poly 1.6g); PROTEIN 28.6g; CARB 24.7g; FIBER 1.8g; CHOL 109mg; IRON 2.8mg; SODIUM 398mg; CALC 59mg

Braised Turkey and Asian Vegetables

Five-spice powder–dusted turkey thighs become tender and moist from slow cooking atop a medley of Asian vegetables. Wheat-flour udon noodles are a perfect complement to the flavorful broth.

Yield: 8 servings (serving size: 5 ounces turkey, ¾ cup vegetable-broth mixture, and 1 tablespoon green onions)

2 (3½-ounce) packages shiitake mushrooms

1 cup thinly sliced red bell pepper

5 baby bok choy, quartered lengthwise

1 (15-ounce) can precut baby corn, drained

1 (8-ounce) can sliced bamboo shoots, drained

2 tablespoons hoisin sauce

2 tablespoons oyster sauce

1 tablespoon lower-sodium soy sauce

2 teaspoons grated peeled fresh ginger

2 teaspoons dark sesame oil

3 garlic cloves, minced

1 tablespoon canola oil

4 bone-in turkey thighs (about 4 pounds), skinned

1 teaspoon five-spice powder

½ teaspoon freshly ground black pepper

2 cups thinly sliced napa (Chinese) cabbage

½ cup chopped green onions

1. Remove stems from mushrooms; slice mushrooms. Place mushrooms, bell pepper, and next 3 ingredients (through bamboo shoots) in a 7-quart electric slow cooker. Combine hoisin sauce and next 5 ingredients (through garlic) in a small bowl. Stir into vegetable mixture in slow cooker.

2. Heat a large nonstick skillet over medium-high heat. Add canola oil to pan; swirl to coat. Sprinkle turkey thighs evenly with five-spice powder and black pepper. Add half of turkey to pan. Cook 3 minutes on each side or until browned. Add turkey to slow cooker. Repeat procedure with remaining turkey. Cover and cook on LOW for 5 hours or until turkey is tender.

3. Remove turkey from bones; cut meat into bite-sized pieces. Discard bones. Stir cabbage into vegetable mixture. Serve vegetables and broth in individual bowls. Top with turkey; sprinkle evenly with green onions.

CALORIES 249; FAT 7.4g (sat 1.7g, mono 2.5g, poly 2.3g); PROTEIN 32.6g; CARB 11.3g; FIBER 2.6g; CHOL 116mg; IRON 3.7mg; SODIUM 466mg; CALC 143mg

Chicken Enchilada Stack

Think outside the "dish." You can enjoy the flavor and texture of enchiladas in a slow cooker; just stack the tortillas instead of rolling them. We suggest lining your slow cooker with a slow-cooker bag so you can easily remove the stack from the cooker.

Yield: 8 servings (serving size: 1 wedge)

1 teaspoon canola oil

1 cup chopped onion

½ cup chopped seeded poblano chile

2 garlic cloves, minced

1½ teaspoons chipotle chile powder

1 (14.5-ounce) can no-salt-added diced tomatoes, drained

1 (8-ounce) can tomato sauce with basil, garlic, and oregano

Cooking spray

2 cups shredded rotisserie chicken breast

1 cup frozen baby white and yellow corn

1 (15-ounce) can black beans, rinsed and drained

5 (8-inch) corn and flour blend tortillas

8 ounces shredded reduced-fat sharp cheddar cheese (about 2 cups)

Cilantro sprigs (optional)

1. Heat a large nonstick skillet over medium-high heat. Add oil to pan; swirl to coat. Add onion, poblano chile, and garlic to pan; cook 6 minutes or until vegetables are tender, stirring frequently.

2. Stir in chile powder, tomatoes, and tomato sauce. Place half of tomato mixture in a blender. Remove center piece of blender lid (to allow steam to escape); secure blender lid on blender. Place a clean towel over opening in blender lid (to avoid splatters). Blend until almost smooth. Pour into a large bowl. Repeat procedure with remaining tomato mixture.

3. Coat a 5-quart round electric slow cooker with cooking spray; place 3 tablespoons tomato mixture in bottom of slow cooker. Combine remaining tomato mixture, chicken, corn, and beans.

4. Place one tortilla on sauce in slow cooker; pour 1 cup chicken mixture over tortilla; sprinkle with ⅓ cup cheese. Top with another tortilla. Repeat procedure with remaining chicken mixture, tortillas, and cheese. Cover and cook on LOW for 2 hours or until cheese melts and edges are lightly browned. Garnish with cilantro, if desired. Cut into 8 wedges.

CALORIES 295; FAT 10.3g (sat 5g, mono 3.9g, poly 1.1g); PROTEIN 24g; CARB 30.5g; FIBER 3.9g; CHOL 55mg; IRON 2.3mg; SODIUM 764mg; CALC 275mg

Chicken Cacciatore

The Italian word "cacciatore" translates to "hunter" in English, referring to a dish prepared with tomatoes, mushrooms, and onions—"hunter-style."

Yield: 8 servings (serving size: 1 thigh and 1 drumstick, about 1 cup vegetable mixture, and ½ cup pasta)

8 bone-in chicken thighs (2¼ pounds), skinned

8 bone-in chicken drumsticks (1¾ pounds), skinned

½ teaspoon salt, divided

½ teaspoon freshly ground black pepper

1 tablespoon olive oil

Cooking spray

1 (8-ounce) package mushrooms, quartered

2 tablespoons minced garlic

1 large onion, sliced

1 green bell pepper, vertically sliced

1 red bell pepper, vertically sliced

½ cup dry white wine

1.5 ounces all-purpose flour (about ⅓ cup)

2 tablespoons chopped fresh oregano

2 tablespoons chopped fresh thyme

1 (28-ounce) can whole plum tomatoes, undrained and chopped

4 cups hot cooked fettuccine

Chopped fresh thyme (optional)

1. Sprinkle chicken with ¼ teaspoon salt and pepper. Heat a large nonstick skillet over medium-high heat. Add oil to pan; swirl to coat. Add half of chicken to pan; cook 5 minutes on each side or until lightly browned. Place chicken in a 5-quart electric slow cooker coated with cooking spray. Repeat procedure with remaining chicken. Place mushrooms on top of chicken.

2. Add garlic, onion, and bell peppers to pan; sprinkle vegetables with remaining ¼ teaspoon salt. Reduce heat to medium, and cook 5 minutes or until vegetables are crisp-tender, stirring often. Add wine, scraping pan to loosen brown bits. Cook 1 minute. Stir in flour. Stir in oregano, thyme, and tomatoes.

3. Pour tomato mixture over mushrooms in slow cooker. Cover and cook on LOW for 3 hours or until chicken is very tender. Serve over fettuccine. Sprinkle with additional thyme, if desired.

CALORIES 361; FAT 7.6g (sat 1.7g, mono 2.9g, poly 1.7g); PROTEIN 32.5g; CARB 35.6g; FIBER 3.4g; CHOL 106mg; IRON 3.5mg; SODIUM 476mg; CALC 59mg

Sesame-Ginger Chicken

Serve over steamed rice to savor every bit of the sweet Asian glaze.

Yield: 4 servings (serving size: 2 chicken thighs, ⅓ cup sauce, ½ teaspoon sesame seeds, and 1½ teaspoons green onions)

1 tablespoon sesame oil

8 bone-in chicken thighs
(2¾ pounds), skinned

Cooking spray

¼ cup lower-sodium soy sauce

2 tablespoons light brown sugar

2 tablespoons fresh orange juice

5 teaspoons hoisin sauce

1 tablespoon minced peeled fresh ginger

1 teaspoon minced garlic

1 tablespoon cornstarch

1 tablespoon cold water

2 teaspoons toasted sesame seeds

2 tablespoons sliced green onions

1. Heat a large nonstick skillet over medium high heat. Add oil to pan; swirl to coat. Add chicken; cook 4 minutes on each side or until golden. Transfer chicken to a 4-quart electric slow cooker coated with cooking spray.

2. Combine soy sauce and next 5 ingredients (through garlic); pour over chicken. Cover and cook on LOW for 2½ hours or until chicken is tender. Transfer chicken to a platter; keep warm.

3. Pour cooking liquid through a sieve into a small saucepan to measure 1¼ cups. Discard solids. Bring cooking liquid to a boil over medium-high heat. Combine cornstarch and 1 tablespoon cold water in a small bowl. Add cornstarch mixture to sauce, stirring with a whisk until blended. Return to a boil. Cook 1 minute or until sauce thickens, stirring constantly. Serve sauce over chicken. Sprinkle with sesame seeds and green onions.

CALORIES 310; FAT 11.6g (sat 2.4g, mono 4g, poly 3.6g); PROTEIN 36.7g; CARB 12g; FIBER 0.6g; CHOL 148mg; IRON 2.3mg; SODIUM 656mg; CALC 34mg

Chicken Verde

Make your friends "green" with envy at your slow cooker savvy by serving up this savory Southwestern-style entrée, loaded with tomatillos, onion, and roasted poblano and jalapeño peppers. Corn tortillas and a simple green salad round out the menu.

Yield: 6 servings (serving size: 1 chicken breast half, ¾ cup sauce, and about 1 tablespoon cilantro)

5 poblano chiles (about ¾ pound)

4 jalapeño peppers (about 4½ ounces)

5½ cups chopped tomatillos (about 1¾ pounds; about 16 small)

2 cups chopped onion (1 large)

1 tablespoon sugar

5 garlic cloves, minced

1 (4.5-ounce) can chopped green chiles, undrained

6 (8-ounce) bone-in chicken breast halves, skinned

1½ teaspoons ground cumin

½ teaspoon freshly ground black pepper

1 tablespoon canola oil

¼ cup chopped fresh cilantro

⅓ cup reduced-fat sour cream (optional)

1. Preheat broiler.

2. Place poblano chiles and jalapeño peppers on a foil-lined baking sheet. Broil 10 minutes or until blackened and charred, turning occasionally. Place peppers in a paper bag; fold to close tightly. Let stand 15 minutes. Peel chiles and peppers; cut in half lengthwise. Discard seeds and membranes. Chop poblano chiles. Finely chop jalapeño peppers.

3. Combine poblano chiles, jalapeño peppers, tomatillos, and next 4 ingredients (through green chiles) in a large bowl.

4. Sprinkle chicken with cumin and pepper. Heat a large nonstick skillet over medium-high heat. Add oil to pan; swirl to coat. Add half of chicken to pan. Cook 2½ minutes on each side or until browned. Place chicken in a 6-quart electric slow cooker. Repeat procedure with remaining chicken. Pour tomatillo mixture over chicken. Cover and cook on LOW for 3½ hours or until chicken is tender.

5. Remove chicken from slow cooker; keep warm. Pour sauce into a medium saucepan. Bring to a boil; reduce heat, and simmer, uncovered, 25 minutes or until reduced to 4½ cups.

6. Serve chicken with sauce. Sprinkle with chopped cilantro. Garnish with sour cream, if desired.

CALORIES 282; FAT 6g (sat 0.9g, mono 2.1g, poly 1.7g); PROTEIN 37.1g; CARB 20.6g; FIBER 5g; CHOL 86mg; IRON 2.4mg; SODIUM 168mg; CALC 55mg

Chicken and Shrimp Jambalaya

Get ready to serve a crowd! Baguette pieces continue the French-Cajun theme.

Yield: 8 servings (serving size: 1¼ cups)

1 tablespoon canola oil

1 pound skinless, boneless chicken breasts, cut into 1-inch pieces

¾ pound skinless, boneless chicken thighs, cut into 1-inch pieces

2 cups chopped onion

1 cup chopped green bell pepper

1 cup chopped celery

2 garlic cloves, minced

4 ounces turkey kielbasa, halved and cut into ¼-inch-thick slices

2 teaspoons salt-free Cajun seasoning

½ teaspoon dried thyme

¼ teaspoon Spanish smoked paprika (optional)

2 (14½-ounce) cans diced tomatoes with onion and green peppers, undrained

1 (14-ounce) can fat-free, lower-sodium chicken broth

2 (3½-ounce) bags boil-in-bag long-grain rice

1 pound medium shrimp, peeled and deveined

2 tablespoons chopped fresh flat-leaf parsley

1 tablespoon hot sauce

Fresh parsley leaves (optional)

1. Heat a large skillet over high heat. Add oil to pan; swirl to coat. Add chicken; cook 4 minutes, stirring occasionally. Place chicken in an electric slow cooker.

2. Add onion, bell pepper, celery, and garlic to pan; sauté 4 minutes or until tender. Add onion mixture, turkey kielbasa, and next 5 ingredients (through chicken broth) to slow cooker. Cover and cook on LOW for 5 hours.

3. Cook rice according to package directions. Add cooked rice and remaining ingredients except parsley garnish to slow cooker. Cover and cook on HIGH 15 minutes or until shrimp are done. Garnish with parsley leaves, if desired.

CALORIES 373; FAT 6.4g (sat 1.4g, mono 2.4g, poly 1.7g); PROTEIN 39.7g; CARB 37.1g; FIBER 3.9g; CHOL 158mg; IRON 5.6mg; SODIUM 660mg; CALC 117mg

Provençale Chicken Supper

Use bone-in chicken breasts for this French-country dish.

Yield: 4 servings (serving size: 1 chicken breast half and 1 cup bean mixture)

4 (6-ounce) chicken breast halves, skinned

2 teaspoons dried basil

⅛ teaspoon salt

⅛ teaspoon freshly ground black pepper

1 cup diced yellow bell pepper

1 (15.5-ounce) can cannellini beans or other white beans, rinsed and drained

1 (14.5-ounce) can diced tomatoes with basil, garlic, and oregano, undrained

Basil sprigs (optional)

1. Place chicken in an electric slow cooker; sprinkle with basil, salt, and black pepper. Add bell pepper, beans, and tomatoes. Cover and cook on LOW for 8 hours. Garnish with basil sprigs, if desired.

CALORIES 281; FAT 2.2g (sat 0.6g, mono 0.5g, poly 0.5g); PROTEIN 44.9g; CARB 18.1g; FIBER 4.7g; CHOL 99mg; IRON 3.2mg; SODIUM 495mg; CALC 86mg

SUBSTITUTION TIP

The flavor of fresh herbs is generally better than dried, but we've used dried basil here for convenience. If you prefer fresh, use 2 tablespoons instead and stir it in at the end.

Lemon-Rosemary Chicken

Five ingredients and ten minutes is all it takes to prep this citrusy chicken for dinner.

Yield: 4 servings (serving size: ¼ of chicken)

2 tablespoons butter, softened

2 tablespoons chopped fresh rosemary

2 garlic cloves, minced

¼ teaspoon salt

¼ teaspoon freshly ground black pepper

1 (4-pound) whole chicken

1 lemon, cut in half crosswise

1. Combine first 5 ingredients in a small bowl.

2. Remove and discard giblets and neck from chicken. Trim excess fat. Starting at neck cavity, loosen skin from breast and drumsticks by inserting fingers, gently pushing between skin and meat. Rub butter mixture under loosened skin and rub over breast and drumsticks. Lift wing tips up and over back; tuck under chicken. Place lemon halves inside cavity.

3. Place chicken, breast side up, on a small rack. Place rack inside slow cooker. Cover and cook on HIGH for 3 hours or until a thermometer inserted into thigh registers 165° to 170°.

CALORIES 315; FAT 12.1g (sat 5.2g, mono 3.4g, poly 1.8g); PROTEIN 47.2g; CARB 2.1g; FIBER 0.7g; CHOL 166mg; IRON 2.5mg; SODIUM 362mg; CALC 36mg

FLAVOR TIP

Rosemary is one of the most aromatic and pungent of all herbs. Its needlelike leaves have a pronounced lemon-pine flavor.

Chicken with Carrots and Potatoes

All you need is twenty minutes to get this dish in the slow cooker. You'll have a hearty chicken and veggie supper waiting for you when you get home.

Yield: 6 servings

1¾ cups vertically sliced onion

Cooking spray

2 cups baby carrots

6 small round red potatoes (about 1 pound), cut into ¼-inch slices

½ cup fat-free, lower-sodium chicken broth

½ cup dry white wine

1 tablespoon chopped fresh thyme

1 teaspoon minced garlic

¾ teaspoon salt, divided

½ teaspoon freshly ground black pepper, divided

1 teaspoon paprika

6 (6-ounce) bone-in chicken thighs, skinned

1 teaspoon olive oil

Chopped fresh thyme (optional)

1. Place onion in a 6-quart electric slow cooker coated with cooking spray; top with carrots and potatoes.
2. Combine broth, next 3 ingredients, ½ teaspoon salt, and ¼ teaspoon pepper. Pour over vegetables.
3. Combine paprika, remaining ¼ teaspoon salt, and remaining ¼ teaspoon pepper; rub over chicken. Heat a large nonstick skillet over medium-high heat. Add oil to pan; swirl to coat. Add chicken. Cook 3 minutes on each side or until browned. Arrange chicken on top of vegetables.
4. Cover and cook on LOW for 3½ hours or until chicken is done and vegetables are tender. Garnish with additional thyme, if desired.

CALORIES 229; FAT 4.9g (sat 1.1g, mono 1.7g, poly 1.1g); PROTEIN 21.7g; CARB 20.7g; FIBER 3.2g; CHOL 80mg; IRON 2.6mg; SODIUM 454mg; CALC 51mg

Pulled Chicken Sandwiches

Yield: 8 servings (serving size: 1 sandwich)

3 cups thinly sliced onion

1 teaspoon canola oil

1¾ pounds skinless, boneless chicken breast halves

1 cup ketchup

2 tablespoons cider vinegar

2 tablespoons molasses

1 tablespoon Dijon mustard

1 teaspoon onion powder

1 teaspoon ground cumin

½ teaspoon garlic powder

½ teaspoon hot sauce

8 (1.2-ounce) whole-wheat hamburger buns, toasted

1. Place onion a 4-quart oval electric slow cooker. Heat a large nonstick skillet over medium-high heat. Add oil to pan; swirl to coat. Add half of chicken, and cook 3 to 4 minutes on each side or until golden brown. Place chicken in a single layer on top of onion. Repeat procedure with remaining chicken.

2. Combine ketchup and next 7 ingredients (through hot sauce); pour over chicken. Cover and cook on LOW for 4 hours until chicken is tender and sauce is thick.

3. Remove chicken from slow cooker. Shred chicken with 2 forks, and stir into sauce. Spoon ¾ cup chicken mixture onto bottom of each bun; cover with bun tops.

CALORIES 271; FAT 3.6g (sat 0.7g, mono 1.1g, poly 1.2g); PROTEIN 27g; CARB 33.6g; FIBER 3.6g; CHOL 58mg; IRON 2.1mg; SODIUM 613mg; CALC 76mg

Provençale Chicken Supper

Use bone-in chicken breasts for this French-country dish.

Yield: 4 servings (serving size: 1 chicken breast half and 1 cup bean mixture)

4 (6-ounce) chicken breast halves, skinned

2 teaspoons dried basil

⅛ teaspoon salt

⅛ teaspoon freshly ground black pepper

1 cup diced yellow bell pepper

1 (15.5-ounce) can cannellini beans or other white beans, rinsed and drained

1 (14.5-ounce) can diced tomatoes with basil, garlic, and oregano, undrained

Basil sprigs (optional)

1. Place chicken in an electric slow cooker; sprinkle with basil, salt, and black pepper. Add bell pepper, beans, and tomatoes. Cover and cook on LOW for 8 hours. Garnish with basil sprigs, if desired.

CALORIES 281; FAT 2.2g (sat 0.6g, mono 0.5g, poly 0.5g); PROTEIN 44.9g; CARB 18.1g; FIBER 4.7g; CHOL 99mg; IRON 3.2mg; SODIUM 495mg; CALC 86mg

SUBSTITUTION TIP

The flavor of fresh herbs is generally better than dried, but we've used dried basil here for convenience. If you prefer fresh, use 2 tablespoons instead and stir it in at the end.

Sweet Glazed Chicken Thighs

Yield: 6 servings (serving size: ½ cup rice, 1 chicken thigh, about ⅓ cup sauce, and 1½ teaspoons green onions)

2 pounds skinless, boneless chicken thighs

½ teaspoon freshly ground black pepper

¼ teaspoon salt

1 teaspoon olive oil

Cooking spray

1 cup pineapple juice

2 tablespoons light brown sugar

2 tablespoons lower-sodium soy sauce

3 tablespoons water

2 tablespoons cornstarch

3 cups hot cooked rice

3 tablespoons sliced green onions

1. Sprinkle chicken with pepper and salt. Heat a large nonstick skillet over medium-high heat. Add oil to pan; swirl to coat. Add chicken to pan. Cook 2 to 3 minutes on each side or until browned. Transfer chicken to a 4-quart electric slow cooker coated with cooking spray. Stir pineapple juice into drippings, scraping pan to loosen browned bits. Remove from heat; stir in brown sugar and soy sauce. Pour juice mixture over chicken. Cover and cook on LOW for 2½ hours.

2. Transfer chicken to a serving platter with a slotted spoon. Increase heat to HIGH. Combine 3 tablespoons water and cornstarch in a small bowl; add to sauce in slow cooker, stirring with a whisk. Cook 2 minutes or until sauce thickens, stirring constantly with whisk.

3. Place rice on each of 6 plates. Top with chicken thighs and sauce. Sprinkle each serving with green onions.

CALORIES 339; FAT 7.1g (sat 1.7g, mono 2.5g, poly 1.6g); PROTEIN 32.4g; CARB 33.7g; FIBER 0.6g; CHOL 125mg; IRON 2.8mg; SODIUM 363mg; CALC 35mg

Old-Fashioned Chicken Fricassee

A classic stew with chicken breasts simmering in white wine and vegetables is sure to bring comfort to your table. (Pictured on page 118)

Yield: 4 servings (serving size: 1 chicken breast half, ⅔ cup sauce, and 1 tablespoon parsley)

3 tablespoons all-purpose flour

1 teaspoon paprika

1 teaspoon poultry seasoning

½ teaspoon salt

½ teaspoon freshly ground black pepper

4 (6-ounce) chicken breast halves, skinned

2 teaspoons butter

2 cups sliced carrot

1½ cups chopped onion

½ cup chopped celery

3 garlic cloves, minced

1 cup fat-free, lower-sodium chicken broth

¼ cup dry white wine

¼ cup chopped fresh parsley

1. Combine first 5 ingredients in a large heavy-duty zip-top plastic bag. Add chicken; seal bag, and toss to coat. Remove chicken from bag, shaking off excess flour. Reserve flour mixture.

2. Melt butter in a large nonstick skillet over medium-high heat until it melts. Add chicken, skinned side down; cook 5 minutes or until chicken is browned, turning after 3 minutes. Remove chicken from pan. Place chicken in a 4-quart oval electric slow cooker.

3. Add carrot, onion, celery, and garlic to slow cooker. Combine reserved flour mixture, broth, and wine in a medium bowl, stirring with a whisk until blended. Add to slow cooker. Cover and cook on LOW for 3 hours or until chicken is tender. Serve chicken with sauce, and sprinkle with parsley.

CALORIES 262; FAT 4g (sat 1.7g, mono 0.9g, poly 0.6g); PROTEIN 34.5g; CARB 18.5g; FIBER 3.5g; CHOL 84mg; IRON 2.2mg; SODIUM 595mg; CALC 70mg

Saucy Chicken over Rice

Yield: 6 servings (serving size: ½ cup rice, 1 drumstick, 1 thigh, and about ½ cup sauce)

6 skinned chicken thighs (about 2 pounds)

6 skinned chicken drumsticks (about 1¾ pounds)

1 teaspoon canola oil

⅓ cup finely chopped onion

2 garlic cloves, minced

⅓ cup dry white wine

1 (14½-ounce) can stewed tomatoes, undrained and chopped

½ teaspoon dried Italian seasoning

½ teaspoon salt-free lemon-herb seasoning

¼ teaspoon salt

¼ teaspoon dried tarragon

¼ teaspoon crushed red pepper

3 cups hot cooked rice

1. Trim fat from chicken. Heat a large nonstick skillet over medium-high heat. Add oil to pan; swirl to coat. Add half of chicken; cook 5 to 7 minutes or until browned, turning occasionally. Place chicken in a 5-quart electric slow cooker. Repeat procedure with remaining chicken.

2. Add onion and garlic to pan; sauté 2 minutes. Add wine, scraping pan to loosen browned bits. Add tomatoes; remove from heat. Stir in Italian seasoning and next 4 ingredients (through red pepper). Pour tomato mixture over chicken in slow cooker. Cover and cook on LOW for 5 hours. Serve chicken and tomato sauce over rice.

CALORIES 405; FAT 8.9g (sat 2.2g, mono 3g, poly 2.3g); PROTEIN 47.1g; CARB 28.3g; FIBER 1.7g; CHOL 173mg; IRON 4.1mg; SODIUM 487mg; CALC 49mg

Herb and Sausage–Stuffed Peppers

You can set up this recipe in less than fifteen minutes, turn on the slow cooker, and go. Come back in four hours, and your supper will be ready.

Yield: 4 servings (serving size: 1 stuffed pepper)

¾ cup water

½ cup uncooked couscous

2 (4-ounce) links spicy turkey Italian sausage

½ teaspoon kosher salt, divided

¼ teaspoon freshly ground black pepper

½ cup crumbled garlic-and-herb goat cheese, divided

4 small red bell peppers (about 1½ pounds)

2 tablespoons sliced fresh basil (optional)

1. Bring ¾ cup water to a boil in a small saucepan; gradually stir in couscous. Remove from heat; cover and let stand 5 minutes. Fluff with a fork.

2. While couscous stands, remove casings from sausage. Cook sausage in a medium nonstick skillet over medium-high heat 4 minutes or until browned, stirring to crumble. Remove from heat. Stir in couscous, ¼ teaspoon salt, and pepper. Stir in 6 tablespoons cheese.

3. Cut tops off bell peppers; reserve tops. Discard seeds and membranes. Sprinkle remaining ¼ teaspoon salt evenly inside peppers. Divide sausage mixture evenly among peppers. Replace tops of peppers. Place stuffed peppers in a 5-quart round electric slow cooker. Cover and cook on LOW for 4 hours or until peppers are tender.

4. Top peppers evenly with remaining 2 tablespoons cheese and, if desired, sprinkle evenly with basil.

CALORIES 299; FAT 12.7g (sat 5.5g, mono 3.4g, poly 1.7g); PROTEIN 18g; CARB 28.8g; FIBER 4.6g; CHOL 44mg; IRON 2mg; SODIUM 625mg; CALC 45mg

meatless
main dishes

Maple-Hazelnut Oatmeal

Yield: 4 servings (serving size: 1¼ cups oatmeal, 1 tablespoon syrup, and ¼ cup hazelnuts)

1½ cups fat-free milk

1½ cups water

Cooking spray

2 Gala apples, peeled and cut into ½-inch cubes (about 3 cups)

1 cup uncooked steel-cut oats

2 tablespoons brown sugar

1½ tablespoons butter, softened

¼ teaspoon ground cinnamon

¼ teaspoon salt

¼ cup maple syrup

1 cup hazelnuts, chopped

1. Bring milk and 1½ cups water to a boil in a saucepan over medium-high heat, stirring frequently.

2. Coat a 3½-quart electric slow cooker with cooking spray. Place hot milk mixture, apple, and next 5 ingredients (through salt) in slow cooker; stir well. Cover and cook on LOW for 7 hours or until oats are tender.

3. Spoon oatmeal into bowls; top with maple syrup and hazelnuts.

CALORIES 283; FAT 8g (sat 3.2g, mono 3.3g, poly 1g); PROTEIN 6.4g; CARB 49g; FIBER 3.4g; CHOL 13mg; IRON 1.5mg; SODIUM 218mg; CALC 145mg

Barley-Stuffed Cabbage Rolls with Pine Nuts and Currants

This dish works well assembled the night before, so a little planning gives you a great head start on the next day's dinner. Trimming away part of the thick center vein from the cabbage leaves makes them more pliable and easier to roll up. Try stirring in one cup thawed frozen meatless crumbles in place of or in addition to the feta cheese. You can also cook the rolls on LOW for four to six hours.

Yield: 4 servings (serving size: 4 cabbage rolls and 2 tablespoons sauce)

1 large head green cabbage, cored

1 tablespoon olive oil

1½ cups finely chopped onion

3 cups cooked pearl barley

3 ounces crumbled feta cheese (about ¾ cup)

½ cup dried currants

2 tablespoons pine nuts, toasted

2 tablespoons chopped fresh parsley

¼ teaspoon salt, divided

¼ teaspoon freshly ground black pepper, divided

½ cup apple juice

1 tablespoon cider vinegar

1 (14.5-ounce) can crushed tomatoes, undrained

1. Steam cabbage head 8 minutes; cool slightly. Remove 16 leaves from cabbage head; discard remaining cabbage. Cut off raised portion of center vein of each cabbage leaf (do not cut out vein); set trimmed cabbage leaves aside.

2. Heat a large nonstick skillet over medium heat. Add oil to pan; swirl to coat. Add onion; cover and cook 6 minutes or until tender. Remove from heat; stir in barley and next 4 ingredients (through parsley). Stir in ⅛ teaspoon salt and ⅛ teaspoon pepper.

3. Place cabbage leaves on a flat surface; spoon about ⅓ cup barley mixture into center of each cabbage leaf. Fold in edges of leaves over barley mixture; roll up. Arrange cabbage rolls in bottom of a 5-quart electric slow cooker.

4. Combine remaining ⅛ teaspoon salt, remaining ⅛ teaspoon pepper, apple juice, vinegar, and tomatoes; pour evenly over cabbage rolls. Cover and cook on HIGH for 2 hours or until thoroughly heated. Serve rolls with sauce.

CALORIES 479; FAT 13.5g (sat 5.2g, mono 4.7g, poly 2.4g); PROTEIN 14.4g; CARB 83.2g; FIBER 16.8g; CHOL 25mg; IRON 5.7mg; SODIUM 661mg; CALC 347mg

Cuban Beans and Rice

Dried beans are inexpensive and a convenient choice for economical meals. They also lend themselves well to slow cooking because, unlike on the cooktop, there is no risk of burning during the long simmering period. This meatless entrée reheats well the next day for lunch. Store leftover bean mixture and rice in separate containers in the refrigerator.

Yield: 10 servings (serving size: 1 cup bean mixture and ½ cup rice)

1 pound dried black beans

2 cups water

2 cups organic vegetable broth

2 cups chopped onion

1½ cups chopped red bell pepper

1 cup chopped green bell pepper

2 tablespoons olive oil

1½ teaspoons salt

2 teaspoons fennel seeds, crushed

2 teaspoons ground coriander

2 teaspoons ground cumin

2 teaspoons dried oregano

2 tablespoons sherry or red wine vinegar

2 (10-ounce) cans diced tomatoes and green chiles, drained

5 cups hot cooked rice

Hot sauce (optional)

1. Sort and wash beans; place in a large bowl. Cover with water to 2 inches above beans; cover and let stand 8 hours. Drain beans.

2. Place beans, 2 cups water, and next 10 ingredients (through oregano) in an electric slow cooker; stir well. Cover and cook on HIGH for 5 hours or until beans are tender. Stir in vinegar and tomatoes. Serve over rice. Sprinkle with hot sauce, if desired.

CALORIES 314; FAT 3.3g (sat 0.5g, mono 2.1g, poly 0.4g); PROTEIN 12g; CARB 57.2g; FIBER 6.2g; CHOL 0mg; IRON 3.8mg; SODIUM 584mg; CALC 33mg

Barley, Black Bean, and Corn Burritos

Loaded with grains and vegetables, these burritos make a complete one-dish meal.

Yield: 8 servings (serving size: 1 burrito)

2 cups fat-free, lower-sodium organic vegetable broth or chicken broth

1 cup uncooked pearl barley

¾ cup frozen whole-kernel corn

¼ cup chopped green onions

1 tablespoon fresh lime juice

1 teaspoon ground cumin

1 teaspoon chili powder

½ teaspoon ground red pepper

1 (15-ounce) can lower-sodium black beans, rinsed and drained

1 (10-ounce) can diced tomatoes and green chiles, undrained

1 garlic clove, minced

¼ cup chopped fresh cilantro

8 (8-inch) flour tortillas

3 ounces shredded reduced-fat sharp cheddar cheese (about ¾ cup)

8 cups thinly sliced curly leaf lettuce

½ cup bottled salsa

½ cup light sour cream

Chopped fresh cilantro (optional)

1. Place first 11 ingredients in a 3- to 4-quart electric slow cooker; stir well. Cover and cook on LOW for 4 hours or until barley is tender and liquid is absorbed. Stir in ¼ cup cilantro.

2. Heat tortillas according to package directions. Spoon ⅔ cup barley mixture down center of each tortilla. Sprinkle each with 1½ tablespoons cheese; roll up. Place 1 cup lettuce on each of 8 plates; top each with 1 burrito. Spoon 1 tablespoon salsa and 1 tablespoon sour cream over each serving. Sprinkle with additional cilantro, if desired.

CALORIES 351; FAT 7.1g (sat 2.8g, mono 2.3g, poly 0.8g); PROTEIN 13.5g; CARB 60.1g; FIBER 7.4g; CHOL 8mg; IRON 2.3mg; SODIUM 740mg; CALC 211mg

Thyme-Scented White Bean Cassoulet

Butter-tossed breadcrumbs stirred in at the end give this dish a robust, stewlike consistency. Meatless Italian sausage stands in for the traditional pork sausage. With this recipe, you can also sauté the sausage in a nonstick skillet over medium-high heat until browned, and then stir it in.

Yield: 6 servings (serving size: 1⅓ cups)

1 tablespoon olive oil

1½ cups chopped onion

1½ cups (½-inch-thick) slices diagonally cut carrot

1 cup (½-inch-thick) slices diagonally cut parsnip

2 garlic cloves, minced

3 cups cooked Great Northern beans

¾ cup organic vegetable broth

½ teaspoon dried thyme

¼ teaspoon salt

¼ teaspoon freshly ground black pepper

1 (28-ounce) can diced tomatoes, undrained

1 bay leaf

¼ cup dry breadcrumbs

1 ounce grated fresh Parmesan cheese (about ¼ cup)

2 tablespoons butter, melted

2 links frozen meatless Italian sausage, thawed and chopped

2 tablespoons chopped fresh parsley

1. Heat a large nonstick skillet over medium heat. Add oil to pan; swirl to coat. Add onion, carrot, parsnip, and garlic; cover and cook 5 minutes or until tender.

2. Place vegetable mixture in a 5-quart electric slow cooker. Stir in beans and next 6 ingredients (through bay leaf). Cover and cook on LOW for 8 hours or until vegetables are tender. Discard bay leaf.

3. Combine breadcrumbs, cheese, and butter in a small bowl; toss with a fork until moist. Stir breadcrumb mixture and sausage into bean mixture; sprinkle with parsley.

CALORIES 298; FAT 9.9g (sat 3.9g, mono 3.6g, poly 1.6g); PROTEIN 13.8g; CARB 40.5g; FIBER 10.4g; CHOL 14mg; IRON 3.5mg; SODIUM 709mg; CALC 187mg

Chickpeas in Curried Coconut Broth

Yield: 6 servings (serving size: 1⅓ cups chickpea mixture and 1 cup rice)

2 teaspoons canola oil

1½ cups chopped onion

2 garlic cloves, minced

2 (19-ounce) cans chickpeas (garbanzo beans), rinsed and drained

2 (14.5-ounce) cans no-salt-added diced tomatoes, undrained

1 (13.5-ounce) can light coconut milk

1 tablespoon curry powder

2 tablespoons chopped pickled jalapeño pepper

1 teaspoon salt

½ cup chopped fresh cilantro

6 cups hot cooked basmati rice

1. Heat a large nonstick skillet over medium heat. Add oil to pan; swirl to coat. Add onion and garlic; sauté 5 minutes or until onion is tender. Place onion mixture, chickpeas, and next 5 ingredients (through salt) in a 3½-quart electric slow cooker; stir well. Cover and cook on LOW for 6 to 8 hours. Stir in cilantro. Serve over rice.

CALORIES 369; FAT 4.3g (sat 0.9g, mono 1.4g, poly 1.1g); PROTEIN 10.5g; CARB 71.1g; FIBER 6.4g; CHOL 0mg; IRON 4mg; SODIUM 620mg; CALC 55mg

Hoppin' John

Hoppin' John is said to bring good luck all year when eaten on New Year's Day.

Yield: 6 servings (serving size: 1⅔ cups)

2 (16-ounce) packages frozen black-eyed peas

1¼ cups sliced green onions, divided

2 cups hot water

¾ cup chopped red bell pepper

2 tablespoons minced seeded jalapeño pepper

2 teaspoons hot sauce

¼ teaspoon salt

¼ teaspoon freshly ground black pepper

1 vegetable-flavored or chicken-flavored bouillon cube

1 (14.5-ounce) can diced tomatoes with pepper, celery, and onion, undrained

1 tablespoon tomato paste

⅔ cup uncooked converted rice

1. Place peas, ¾ cup green onions, 2 cups hot water, and next 6 ingredients (through bouillon) in a 4-quart electric slow cooker; stir well. Cover and cook on HIGH for 4 hours. Stir in tomatoes, tomato paste, and rice; cover and cook on HIGH for 1 hour or until peas and rice are tender and most of liquid is absorbed. Stir in remaining ½ cup green onions.

CALORIES 349; FAT 1.5g (sat 0.5g, mono 0.3g, poly 0.7g); PROTEIN 17.6g; CARB 67g; FIBER 11.8g; CHOL 0mg; IRON 4.9mg; SODIUM 632mg; CALC 87mg

Tofu and Chickpea Curry

Experiment with a variety of fresh vegetables in this vegetarian Madras curry. You can stir in spinach or Swiss chard during the last 30 minutes of cooking, if you like.

Yield: 6 servings (serving size: 1½ cups curry, ½ cup rice, and 1½ teaspoons cilantro)

2 cups (¾-inch) cubed peeled sweet potato

2 cups small cauliflower florets

1 cup chopped onion

1 tablespoon Madras curry powder

1 tablespoon brown sugar

1 tablespoon grated peeled fresh ginger

1¼ teaspoons salt

2 garlic cloves, minced

1 (16-ounce) can chickpeas (garbanzo beans), rinsed and drained

1 (14.5-ounce) can no-salt-added diced tomatoes, undrained

1 (13.5-ounce) can light coconut milk

1 (14-ounce) package extra-firm tofu, drained

1 tablespoon canola oil

3 cups hot cooked rice

3 tablespoons chopped fresh cilantro

Freshly ground black pepper (optional)

1. Place first 11 ingredients in a 4-quart electric slow cooker; stir well. Cover and cook on LOW for 5½ hours or until vegetables are tender.

2. Place tofu on several layers of paper towels; cover with additional paper towels. Press to absorb excess moisture; cut into ½-inch cubes.

3. Heat a large nonstick skillet over medium-high heat. Add oil to pan; swirl to coat. Add tofu; cook 8 to 10 minutes or until browned, turning with a spatula. Stir into vegetable mixture in slow cooker. Cover and cook on LOW for 30 minutes.

4. Spoon rice into bowls. Ladle curry evenly over rice. Sprinkle with cilantro and, if desired, black pepper.

CALORIES 328; FAT 7g (sat 1.4g, mono 2.5g, poly 2.8g); PROTEIN 12.8g; CARB 53.8g; FIBER 6.7g; CHOL 0mg; IRON 3.7mg; SODIUM 627mg; CALC 112mg

Spanish Tortilla (*Tortilla de Patatas*)

We recommend using a slow-cooker liner for this recipe and hitting it with some cooking spray before adding the potato mixture. It makes serving and cleanup a cinch.

Yield: 4 servings (serving size: 1 wedge)

2 teaspoons olive oil

2 cups thinly sliced peeled baking potato

1⅓ cups chopped onion

1 cup chopped red bell pepper

Cooking spray

3 large eggs

6 large egg whites

¼ teaspoon salt

½ teaspoon freshly ground black pepper

2 tablespoons grated fresh Parmesan cheese

2 tablespoons chopped fresh parsley

2 tablespoons drained capers

1. Heat a large nonstick skillet over medium-high heat. Add oil to pan; swirl to coat. Add potato, onion, and bell pepper. Cook 8 minutes or until onion is tender and potato just begins to brown, stirring occasionally.

2. Coat a 3-quart electric slow cooker with cooking spray. Place potato mixture in slow cooker. Combine eggs and next 3 ingredients (through black pepper), stirring with a whisk. Pour egg mixture over vegetables in slow cooker. Cover and cook on LOW for 2½ hours or just until egg is set in center.

3. Turn off slow cooker. Let stand, covered, 10 minutes. Sprinkle with cheese, parsley, and capers. Cut into wedges.

CALORIES 200; FAT 7.6g (sat 2.1g, mono 3.5g, poly 0.9g); PROTEIN 15.2g; CARB 28.9g; FIBER 2.7g; CHOL 161mg; IRON 2.3mg; SODIUM 483mg; CALC 109mg

Ratatouille

Serve with any pasta you have on hand. We used penne, but just about any other pasta will do.

Yield: 6 servings (serving size: 1 cup ratatouille, 1 cup pasta, and 2 tablespoons cheese)

2 cups (1-inch) cubed peeled eggplant (about 6 ounces)

1 cup chopped onion

1 cup chopped red bell pepper

⅓ cup dry white wine

½ teaspoon salt

¼ teaspoon freshly ground black pepper

4 garlic cloves, minced

2 medium zucchini, halved lengthwise and sliced

2 medium-sized yellow squash, halved lengthwise and sliced

1 (14.5-ounce) can diced fire-roasted tomatoes, undrained

⅓ cup chopped fresh basil

12 ounces uncooked penne (tube-shaped pasta)

3 ounces crumbled goat cheese (about ¾ cup)

1. Place first 10 ingredients in a 5-quart electric slow cooker; stir well. Cover and cook on LOW for 4 hours or until eggplant is tender. Stir in basil.

2. Cook pasta according to package directions, omitting salt and fat. Serve ratatouille over pasta, and sprinkle with cheese.

CALORIES 336; FAT 5.6g (sat 3.2g, mono 1.1g, poly 0.7g); PROTEIN 13.2g; CARB 55.3g; FIBER 4.9g; CHOL 11mg; IRON 2.1mg; SODIUM 433mg; CALC 91mg

STORAGE TIP

Eggplants are best stored in a cool, dry place (50 degrees is ideal) for one to two days. For longer storage, place whole, unwashed eggplants in a plastic bag in the vegetable drawer of your fridge.

Curried Vegetables on Couscous

This high-flavor dish combines fresh vegetables with curry, cumin, cayenne, and chutney.

Yield: 6 servings (serving size: 1⅔ cups vegetables, ½ cup couscous, 1 tablespoon chutney, 1 tablespoon raisins, and 1 tablespoon yogurt)

4 cups (½-inch) cubed peeled baking potato (about 1½ pounds)

4 cups cubed tomato (about 1½ pounds)

1 cup chopped onion

1 cup (¼-inch) diagonally cut carrot

2 tablespoons curry powder

2 teaspoons cumin seeds

1 teaspoon salt

¼ teaspoon cayenne pepper

2 (15-ounce) cans chickpeas (garbanzo beans), rinsed and drained

1 green bell pepper, cut into ½-inch-wide strips

3 garlic cloves, minced

⅓ cup chopped fresh cilantro

4 green onion tops, cut into 1-inch pieces

3 cups hot cooked couscous

6 tablespoons mango chutney

6 tablespoons raisins

6 tablespoons plain fat-free yogurt

1. Place potato in a 4-quart electric slow cooker. Combine tomato and next 9 ingredients (through garlic) in a bowl; stir well. Spoon over potato. Cover and cook on LOW for 9 hours. Stir in cilantro and green onions. Serve over couscous; top with chutney, raisins, and yogurt.

CALORIES 402; FAT 2.2g (sat 0.3g, mono 0.5g, poly 0.8g); PROTEIN 13.3g; CARB 94.9g; FIBER 10.4g; CHOL 0mg; IRON 4.5mg; SODIUM 773mg; CALC 125mg

Mediterranean Succotash

Traditional Southern succotash is a combination of lima beans, corn, and tomatoes. In our version, Mediterranean vegetables are the stars. (Pictured on page 162)

Yield: 8 servings (serving size: ¾ cup succotash, about ⅔ cup couscous, and 1 tablespoon cheese)

1 cup organic vegetable broth

1 cup chopped zucchini

1 cup chopped red bell pepper

½ cup pitted kalamata olives, halved

2 garlic cloves, minced

2 (15-ounce) cans cannellini beans, rinsed and drained

1 (14.5-ounce) can diced tomatoes, undrained

¼ cup chopped fresh parsley

2 tablespoons balsamic vinegar

2 tablespoons fresh lemon juice

¼ teaspoon freshly ground black pepper

1 (10-ounce) package couscous

2 ounces crumbled feta cheese (about ½ cup)

1. Place first 7 ingredients in a 4-quart electric slow cooker; stir well. Cover and cook on LOW for 4 hours. Stir in parsley and next 3 ingredients (through black pepper).

2. Cook couscous according to package directions, omitting salt and fat. Serve succotash over couscous; sprinkle with cheese.

CALORIES 263; FAT 4.2g (sat 1.4g, mono 2.2g, poly 0.4g); PROTEIN 11g; CARB 45.1g; FIBER 5.8g; CHOL 6mg; IRON 1.9mg; SODIUM 553mg; CALC 117mg

Vegetable Pot Pie with Parmesan–Black Pepper Biscuits

Yield: 8 servings (serving size: about 1½ cups filling and 1 biscuit)

Filling:

2 tablespoons olive oil, divided

2 cups diced peeled baking potato (8 ounces)

1¼ cups diced carrot (3 carrots)

1 cup diced parsnip (2 parsnips)

¾ cup chopped celery (3 stalks)

2 (8-ounce) packages presliced cremini mushrooms

¼ teaspoon salt

½ teaspoon freshly ground black pepper

2 garlic cloves, minced

Cooking spray

2½ tablespoons all-purpose flour

1½ cups 1% low-fat milk

¾ cup organic vegetable broth

2 cups frozen petite green peas

1½ tablespoons chopped fresh thyme

1 (16-ounce) package frozen pearl onions

Biscuit topping:

7.5 ounces all-purpose flour (about 1⅔ cups)

1½ teaspoons baking powder

¾ teaspoon baking soda

⅛ teaspoon salt

1 teaspoon freshly ground black pepper

4½ tablespoons unsalted butter, cut into pieces

2 ounces grated fresh Parmesan cheese (about ½ cup)

3 tablespoons chopped fresh chives

1 cup low-fat buttermilk

1. To prepare filling, heat a large nonstick skillet over medium-high heat. Add 1½ teaspoons oil to pan; swirl to coat. Add potato and next 6 ingredients (through black pepper); sauté 5 minutes. Add garlic; sauté 1 minute. Coat a 5-quart electric slow cooker with cooking spray. Transfer vegetable mixture to slow cooker.

2. Heat remaining 1½ tablespoons oil in pan over medium-high heat. Add 2½ tablespoons flour, stirring with a whisk. Cook 1 minute, whisking constantly. Gradually add milk and broth, stirring with a whisk. Cook over medium heat 3 minutes or until thick and bubbly, stirring constantly with whisk. Pour sauce into slow cooker. Stir in peas, thyme, and onions. Cover and cook on LOW for 3½ hours or until vegetables are tender.

3. To make biscuit topping, weigh or lightly spoon 7.5 ounces flour into dry measuring cups; level with a knife. Combine flour, baking powder, and next 3 ingredients (through black pepper) in a large bowl, stirring with a whisk. Cut in butter with a pastry blender or 2 knives until mixture resembles coarse meal. Stir in cheese and chives. Add buttermilk, stirring just until moist.

4. Increase slow cooker heat to HIGH. Drop biscuits onto filling in 8 equal mounds. Cover and cook on HIGH for 1 hour and 15 minutes or until biscuits are done. Uncover and let stand 5 minutes before serving.

CALORIES 346; FAT 12.7g (sat 6g, mono 4.8g, poly 1g); PROTEIN 11.9g; CARB 48.2g; FIBER 5.4g; CHOL 25mg; IRON 2.8mg; SODIUM 606mg; CALC 243mg

soups
&stews

Potato Soup

This classic soup gets a double hit of cheese—stirred into the soup and sprinkled over the top.

Yield: 8 servings (serving size: about 1 cup soup, 1 tablespoon sour cream, 1½ teaspoons cheese, 1 teaspoon bacon, and ½ teaspoon chives)

3 bacon slices

1 cup chopped onion

3 pounds baking potatoes, peeled and cut into ¼-inch-thick slices

Cooking spray

½ cup water

2 (14.5-ounce) cans fat-free, lower-sodium chicken broth

½ teaspoon salt

½ teaspoon freshly ground black pepper

2 cups 1% low-fat milk

4 ounces shredded reduced-fat sharp cheddar cheese (about 1 cup), divided

½ cup light sour cream

4 teaspoons chopped fresh chives

1. Cook bacon in a large nonstick skillet over medium heat until crisp. Remove bacon from pan, reserving 2 teaspoons drippings in pan; crumble bacon. Add onion to drippings in pan; sauté 3 minutes or until tender.

2. Place potato slices and onion in a 5-quart electric slow cooker coated with cooking spray. Combine ½ cup water and next 3 ingredients (through pepper); stir into mixture in slow cooker. Cover and cook on LOW for 8 hours or until potatoes are tender.

3. Mash mixture with a potato masher; stir in milk and ¾ cup cheese. Increase heat to HIGH. Cover and cook on HIGH for 20 minutes or until mixture is thoroughly heated. Ladle soup into bowls. Top with sour cream and remaining ¼ cup cheese. Sprinkle with bacon and chives.

CALORIES 259; FAT 6.4g (sat 3.9g, mono 2g, poly 0.4g); PROTEIN 13.2g; CARB 37.8g; FIBER 2.6g; CHOL 17mg; IRON 1.6mg; SODIUM 683mg; CALC 202mg

Caribbean Black Bean Soup

A little of this spicy soup goes a long way, so it's best when served as an appetizer soup. If you want to decrease the heat, seed the jalapeños. (Pictured on page 182)

Yield: 8 servings (serving size: about 1 cup soup, 1 tablespoon cilantro, and 1 lime wedge)

1 tablespoon olive oil

2 cups chopped red onion (1 onion)

1 cup diced green bell pepper

1 cup diced red bell pepper

3 tablespoons finely chopped jalapeño pepper (2 peppers)

1 whole garlic head, peeled and minced

¼ cup no-salt-added tomato paste

4 cups organic vegetable broth, divided

1 teaspoon dried thyme

1 teaspoon ground cumin

½ teaspoon ground ginger

½ teaspoon ground allspice

¼ teaspoon ground red pepper

⅛ teaspoon salt

2 (15-ounce) cans no-salt-added black beans, rinsed and drained

½ cup coconut milk

½ cup chopped fresh cilantro

2 limes, quartered

1. Heat a large skillet over medium-high heat. Add oil to pan; swirl to coat. Add onion and next 3 ingredients (through jalapeño); sauté 4 minutes. Add garlic; sauté 1 minute. Stir in tomato paste and 1 cup broth. Transfer vegetable mixture to a 5-quart electric slow cooker.
2. Stir in remaining 3 cups broth, thyme, and next 6 ingredients (through black beans). Cover and cook on LOW for 8 hours.
3. Stir in coconut milk. Ladle soup into bowls; top with cilantro. Serve with lime wedges.

CALORIES 143; FAT 5g (sat 3g, mono 1.4g, poly 0.3g); PROTEIN 5.5g; CARB 20.5g; FIBER 5.6g; CHOL 0mg; IRON 2.3mg; SODIUM 333mg; CALC 59mg

Black Bean Soup

Cumin and fiery serrano chile infuse this simple soup as it cooks; a dollop of sour cream just before it's served provides a refreshing foil for the spiciness. For less heat, seed the chile first or use a milder pepper, such as jalapeño. You can also omit the chile altogether, if you prefer.

Yield: 6 servings

1 pound dried black beans

4 cups organic vegetable broth

2 cups chopped onion

1 cup water

1 tablespoon ground cumin

3 bay leaves

1 serrano chile, finely chopped

2 tablespoons fresh lime juice

1 teaspoon kosher salt

¼ cup chopped fresh cilantro

3 tablespoons reduced-fat sour cream

Cilantro sprigs (optional)

1. Sort and wash beans; place in a large bowl. Cover with water to 2 inches above beans; cover and let stand 8 hours. Drain.

2. Combine beans, broth, and next 5 ingredients (through chile) in an electric slow cooker. Cover and cook on LOW for 10 hours. Discard bay leaves. Stir in juice and salt. Ladle 1½ cups soup into each of 6 bowls; sprinkle each with 2 teaspoons chopped cilantro. Top each serving with 1½ teaspoons sour cream. Garnish with cilantro sprigs, if desired.

CALORIES 286; FAT 2.2g (sat 0.8g, mono 0.4g, poly 0.5g); PROTEIN 17g; CARB 51.1g; FIBER 17.1g; CHOL 3mg; IRON 4.4mg; SODIUM 697mg; CALC 82mg

Three-Bean Vegetarian Chili

This soup has a mild chile flavor. If you want more heat, increase the amount of chili powder and don't seed the jalapeños.

Yield: 8 servings (serving size: 1 cup soup, 1 tablespoon sour cream, 1 tablespoon cheese, and 1½ teaspoons cilantro)

1¾ cups organic vegetable broth

1 cup chopped onion

¼ cup chopped seeded jalapeño pepper (2 peppers)

2 teaspoons chili powder

2 teaspoons ground cumin

2 teaspoons Worcestershire sauce

½ teaspoon salt

2 garlic cloves, minced

2 (15-ounce) cans no-salt-added black beans, rinsed and drained

2 (14.5-ounce) cans diced tomatoes, undrained

1 (15-ounce) can no-salt-added pinto beans, rinsed and drained

1 (15-ounce) can no-salt-added kidney beans, rinsed and drained

½ cup reduced-fat sour cream

2 ounces shredded Monterey Jack cheese with jalapeño peppers (about ½ cup)

¼ cup chopped fresh cilantro

1. Combine first 12 ingredients in a 6-quart electric slow cooker. Cover and cook on LOW for 8 hours.

2. Ladle soup into bowls; top with sour cream, cheese, and cilantro.

CALORIES 197; FAT 3.8g (sat 2.3g, mono 1.1g, poly 0.2g); PROTEIN 11.2g; CARB 28.9g; FIBER 8.9g; CHOL 8mg; IRON 2.8mg; SODIUM 591mg; CALC 129mg

Pinto Bean Chili with Corn and Winter Squash

The spiciness of this light yet filling chili is complemented by the subtle sweetness of corn and winter squash. Queso fresco is a crumbly, slightly salty Mexican cheese that's available in many large supermarkets. If you can't find it, substitute crumbled feta or farmer cheese. For a heartier chili, add one cup thawed frozen meatless crumbles. For a vegan version, use shredded soy cheddar or mozzarella cheese.

Yield: 6 servings (serving size: 1½ cups chili, 2 tablespoons cheese, and 1 lime wedge)

1 tablespoon olive oil

1½ cups chopped onion

1½ cups chopped red bell pepper

1 garlic clove, minced

2 tablespoons chili powder

½ teaspoon ground cumin

2 (12-ounce) packages cubed butternut squash (about 5¼ cups)

3 cups cooked pinto beans

1½ cups water

1 cup frozen whole-kernel corn

1 teaspoon salt

1 (14.5-ounce) can crushed tomatoes, undrained

1 (4.5-ounce) can chopped green chiles, undrained

3 ounces crumbled queso fresco (about ¾ cup)

6 lime wedges

1. Heat a large nonstick skillet over medium heat. Add oil to pan; swirl to coat. Add onion, bell pepper, and garlic; cover and cook 5 minutes or until tender. Add chili powder and cumin; cook 1 minute, stirring constantly.
2. Place onion mixture in a 5-quart electric slow cooker. Stir in butternut squash and next 6 ingredients (through chiles). Cover and cook on LOW for 8 hours or until vegetables are tender and chili is thick. Ladle chili into bowls. Sprinkle with cheese; serve with lime wedges.

CALORIES 320; FAT 5.9g (sat 2.1g, mono 2.6g, poly 0.7g); PROTEIN 15.3g; CARB 55.7g; FIBER 13.6g; CHOL 10mg; IRON 4mg; SODIUM 650mg; CALC 224mg

White Bean, Artichoke, and Chard Ragout

Yield: 6 servings (serving size: 2 cups ragout and about ½ cup relish)

Ragout:

1 tablespoon olive oil

3 cups thinly sliced leek

1 cup (½-inch-thick) slices carrot

3 garlic cloves, minced

3 cups cooked cannellini beans

2½ cups chopped fennel bulb

2 cups (½-inch) cubed red potato

1 cup chopped red bell pepper

¾ cup water

1 teaspoon dried basil

¼ teaspoon salt

¼ teaspoon dried oregano

¼ teaspoon ground black pepper

1 (14.5-ounce) can diced tomatoes with basil, garlic, and oregano, drained

1¾ cups organic vegetable broth

1 (9-ounce) package frozen artichoke hearts, thawed

2 cups chopped Swiss chard

Relish:

1 cup boiling water

6 sun-dried tomatoes, without oil

3 cups shredded fennel bulb

1 cup diced yellow bell pepper

¼ cup chopped fresh parsley

1 tablespoon fresh lemon juice

2 teaspoons olive oil

½ teaspoon sugar

¼ teaspoon salt

⅛ teaspoon ground black pepper

1. To prepare ragout, heat a large nonstick skillet over medium heat. Add 1 tablespoon oil to pan; swirl to coat. Add leek, carrot, and garlic; cover and cook 5 minutes or until tender.

2. Place leek mixture in a 5-quart electric slow cooker. Stir in beans and next 11 ingredients (through artichokes). Cover and cook on HIGH for 8 hours or until vegetables are tender. Add chard; stir until chard wilts.

3. To prepare relish, combine 1 cup boiling water and sun-dried tomatoes; let stand 15 minutes or until soft. Drain; chop. Combine sun-dried tomatoes, shredded fennel, and remaining ingredients; let stand 30 minutes. Serve with ragout.

CALORIES 289; FAT 5.9g (sat 0.8g, mono 2.8g, poly 1.1g); PROTEIN 11.5g; CARB 50.6g; FIBER 13.9g; CHOL 0mg; IRON 4.9mg; SODIUM 603mg; CALC 167mg

Chickpea Chili

Yield: 8 servings (serving size: 1 cup chili, ¾ cup couscous, 1 lime wedge, and 1½ teaspoons cilantro)

1 cup dried chickpeas

2 quarts boiling water

2 tablespoons olive oil, divided

1½ cups chopped onion

5 garlic cloves, minced

1 tablespoon tomato paste

1½ teaspoons ground cumin

½ teaspoon kosher salt

½ teaspoon ground red pepper

½ teaspoon ground cinnamon

¼ teaspoon ground turmeric

2½ cups fat-free, lower-sodium chicken broth

½ cup water

⅔ cup sliced pimiento-stuffed olives

½ cup golden raisins

1 (28-ounce) can whole tomatoes, undrained and crushed

4 cups chopped peeled butternut squash

1 cup frozen green peas, thawed

6 cups hot cooked couscous

8 lime wedges

¼ cup chopped fresh cilantro

1. Place chickpeas in a saucepan; add 2 quarts boiling water. Cover and let stand 1 hour; drain. Place chickpeas in a 6-quart electric slow cooker.
2. Heat a large skillet over medium-high heat. Add 1 tablespoon oil to pan; swirl to coat. Add onion; cook 4 minutes, stirring occasionally. Add garlic; sauté 1 minute. Stir in tomato paste and next 5 ingredients (through turmeric); sauté 30 seconds. Add onion mixture to slow cooker. Stir broth and next 4 ingredients (through tomatoes) into mixture in slow cooker; cover and cook on HIGH for 8 hours.
3. Heat a large skillet over medium-high heat. Add remaining 1 tablespoon oil to pan; swirl to coat. Add squash; sauté 5 minutes. Add squash to slow cooker. Cover and cook on HIGH for 1 hour; stir in peas. Serve over couscous with lime wedges. Sprinkle with cilantro.

CALORIES 386; FAT 6.9g (sat 0.6g, mono 3.6g, poly 1.9g); PROTEIN 13.4g; CARB 70.8g; FIBER 8.4g; CHOL 0mg; IRON 4mg; SODIUM 669mg; CALC 126mg

Curried Lentil-Tomato Soup

Yield: 6 servings (serving size: about 1 cup soup and 2 teaspoons bacon)

4 center-cut bacon slices

1½ cups chopped sweet onion
(1 onion)

4 garlic cloves, finely chopped

3 cups fat-free, lower-sodium
chicken broth

1 cup dried lentils

½ cup chopped carrot

½ cup chopped celery

2 teaspoons curry powder

½ teaspoon ground ginger

¼ teaspoon ground cinnamon

2 (14.5-ounce) cans no-salt-added
stewed tomatoes, undrained

½ cup half-and-half

2 tablespoons dry sherry

1. Cook bacon in a large nonstick skillet over medium heat until crisp. Remove bacon from pan; crumble. Add onion and garlic to drippings in pan; sauté 3 minutes. Transfer onion mixture to a 4-quart electric slow cooker. Stir in broth and next 7 ingredients (through tomatoes). Cover and cook on LOW for 8 hours.
2. Stir in half-and-half and sherry. Ladle soup into bowls; sprinkle with crumbled bacon.

CALORIES 218; FAT 3.7g (sat 1.9g, mono 1.2g, poly 0.4g); PROTEIN 13.5g; CARB 32.8g; FIBER 10.6g; CHOL 11mg; IRON 5mg; SODIUM 445mg; CALC 102mg

Butternut Squash–Parsnip Soup

To serve twelve to sixteen, make two batches of soup instead of doubling the recipe.

Yield: 8 servings (serving size: 1½ cups soup)

2 cups chopped sweet onion
(1 large)

2 cups chopped parsnip (3 large)

1½ cups chopped peeled Granny
Smith apple (about 1 large)

¼ teaspoon salt

1 teaspoon freshly ground black
pepper

3 cups water

2 cups fat-free, lower-sodium
chicken broth

3 (12-ounce) packages frozen
butternut squash, thawed

2 tablespoons whipping cream

⅛ teaspoon paprika

⅛ teaspoon ground cumin

½ cup light sour cream (optional)

8 teaspoons chopped fresh chives
(optional)

1. Combine first 8 ingredients in a 5-quart electric slow cooker. Cover and cook on LOW for 6 hours.

2. Place one-fourth of squash mixture in a blender. Remove center piece of blender lid (to allow steam to escape); secure blender lid on blender. Place a clean towel over opening in blender lid (to avoid splatters). Blend until smooth. Pour into a large bowl. Repeat procedure with remaining squash mixture. Stir in whipping cream, paprika, and cumin. Ladle soup into bowls; top each serving with sour cream and chives, if desired.

CALORIES 132; FAT 1.5g (sat 0.8g, mono 0.4g, poly 0.1g); PROTEIN 3.7g; CARB 29.7g; FIBER 4g; CHOL 4mg; IRON 1.4mg; SODIUM 228mg; CALC 60mg

Curried Squash and Apple Soup

For a main-dish option, add diced cooked chicken or turkey breast to the slow cooker in the last 20 minutes of cooking. Serve garnished with a dollop of sour cream and chopped fresh cilantro.

Yield: 8 servings (serving size: 1 cup)

3 cups fat-free, lower-sodium chicken broth

2 cups chopped onion (about 1 large)

2 teaspoons minced garlic

1½ teaspoons grated peeled fresh ginger

1 teaspoon red curry powder

½ teaspoon salt

½ teaspoon ground coriander

½ teaspoon freshly ground black pepper

3 cups cubed peeled butternut squash (2 pounds)

2 cups diced peeled apple (2 medium)

1. Combine all ingredients in an electric slow cooker. Cover and cook on LOW for 8 hours or until squash is tender.

2. Place half of squash mixture in a blender. Remove center piece of blender lid (to allow steam to escape); secure blender lid on blender. Place a clean towel over opening in blender lid (to avoid splatters). Blend until smooth. Pour pureed mixture into a large bowl. Repeat procedure with remaining squash mixture.

CALORIES 107; FAT 0.5g (sat 0.1g, mono 0.1g, poly 0.1g); PROTEIN 2.7g; CARB 25.2g; FIBER 4.2g; CHOL 0mg; IRON 1.2mg; SODIUM 299mg; CALC 75mg

MAKE-AHEAD TIP

This recipe keeps in the refrigerator for up to four days and up to two months in the freezer.

All-American Beef Stew

A few minutes of effortless prep yield this flavorful classic. Use a blender to dissolve the tapioca completely.

Yield: 6 servings (serving size: about 1¾ cups)

2 tablespoons uncooked granulated tapioca

1 tablespoon sugar

1 tablespoon garlic powder

¼ teaspoon salt

3 (5.5-ounce) cans tomato juice

4 cups chopped onion

3 cups chopped celery

2½ cups (¼-inch-thick) slices carrot

2 (8-ounce) packages presliced mushrooms

2 pounds beef stew meat

Chopped fresh parsley (optional)

1. Place tapioca, sugar, garlic powder, salt, and tomato juice in a blender; process until smooth.

2. Combine onion, celery, carrot, mushrooms, and beef in an electric slow cooker; add juice mixture, stirring well. Cover and cook on HIGH for 5 hours or until beef is tender. Sprinkle with parsley, if desired.

CALORIES 350; FAT 11.7g (sat 4.3g, mono 5g, poly 0.6g); PROTEIN 33.3g; CARB 28.1g; FIBER 4.5g; CHOL 98mg; IRON 4.7mg; SODIUM 510mg; CALC 90mg

Provençal Beef Daube

If you can't find niçoise olives, use another meaty variety, such as kalamata or gaeta.

Yield: 8 servings (serving size: about ¾ cup)

2 pounds boneless chuck roast, trimmed and cut into chunks

1 tablespoon extra-virgin olive oil

6 garlic cloves, minced

½ cup boiling water

½ ounce dried porcini mushrooms

¾ teaspoon salt, divided

Cooking spray

½ cup red wine

¼ cup fat-free, lower-sodium beef broth

⅓ cup pitted niçoise olives

½ teaspoon freshly ground black pepper

2 large carrots, peeled and thinly sliced

1 large onion, peeled and chopped

1 celery stalk, thinly sliced

1 (15-ounce) can whole tomatoes, drained and crushed

1 teaspoon whole black peppercorns

3 flat-leaf parsley sprigs

3 thyme sprigs

1 bay leaf

1 (1-inch) strip orange rind

1 tablespoon water

1 teaspoon cornstarch

1½ tablespoons fresh flat-leaf parsley leaves

1½ teaspoons chopped fresh thyme

1. Combine first 3 ingredients in a large zip-top plastic bag. Seal and marinate at room temperature 30 minutes, turning bag occasionally.
2. Combine ½ cup boiling water and mushrooms; cover and let stand 30 minutes. Drain through a sieve over a bowl, reserving mushrooms and ¼ cup soaking liquid. Chop mushrooms.
3. Heat a large skillet over medium-high heat. Sprinkle beef mixture with ¼ teaspoon salt. Coat pan with cooking spray. Add half of beef mixture to pan; sauté 5 minutes, turning to brown on all sides. Place browned beef mixture in a 6-quart electric slow cooker. Repeat procedure with cooking spray and remaining beef mixture. Add wine and broth to skillet; bring to a boil, scraping pan to loosen browned bits. Pour wine mixture into slow cooker. Add mushrooms, reserved ¼ cup soaking liquid, remaining ½ teaspoon salt, olives, and next 5 ingredients (through tomatoes). Place peppercorns, parsley sprigs, thyme sprigs, bay leaf, and orange rind on a double layer of cheese-cloth. Gather edges of cheesecloth together; tie securely. Add cheesecloth bundle to slow cooker. Cover and cook on LOW for 6 hours or until beef and vegetables are tender. Discard the cheese-cloth bundle.
4. Combine 1 tablespoon water and cornstarch in a small bowl, stirring until smooth. Add cornstarch mixture to slow cooker; cook 20 minutes or until slightly thick, stirring occasionally. Sprinkle with parsley and chopped thyme.

CALORIES 360; FAT 22.5g (sat 8g, mono 10.6g, poly 1.1g); PROTEIN 30.2g; CARB 7.8g; FIBER 2.2g; CHOL 94mg; IRON 3.5mg; SODIUM 516mg; CALC 53mg

Vegetable-Beef Soup

Yield: 8 servings (serving size: about 1¾ cups)

1.1 ounces all-purpose flour (about ¼ cup)

1½ pounds lean top round steak, cut into 1-inch cubes

2 teaspoons spicy herb blend

2 (16-ounce) packages frozen gumbo vegetables mix

1 (10-ounce) package frozen chopped onion

2 (14.5-ounce) cans diced tomatoes with garlic, undrained

2 (14.5-ounce) cans fat-free, lower-sodium beef broth

1 tablespoon minced garlic

1 tablespoon lower-sodium Worcestershire sauce

½ teaspoon salt

½ teaspoon freshly ground black pepper

1. Place flour in a large zip-top plastic bag; add steak cubes. Seal and shake to coat. Remove steak from bag; set aside.

2. Heat a large nonstick skillet over medium-high heat. Cook steak, browning on all sides.

3. Place steak, herb blend, and remaining ingredients in a 4-quart electric slow cooker; stir well. Cover and cook on LOW for 7 hours or until meat is done and vegetables are tender.

CALORIES 248; FAT 5.7g (sat 2g, mono 2.2g, poly 0.3g); PROTEIN 23g; CARB 22g; FIBER 4.1g; CHOL 49mg; IRON 2.7mg; SODIUM 587mg; CALC 26mg

Posole

You'll love the aroma of cumin, oregano, and gently braised pork that will fill your home as the stew cooks.

Yield: 8 servings (serving size: about 1⅓ cups soup, 2 tablespoons slaw, 1 tablespoon radishes, and 1 tablespoon avocado)

1 tablespoon canola oil

2 (1-pound) pork tenderloins, cut into 1½-inch pieces

4 cups fat-free, lower-sodium chicken broth

1⅔ cups chopped onion (about 1 medium)

1½ teaspoons ground cumin

1 teaspoon dried oregano

½ teaspoon freshly ground black pepper

¼ teaspoon ground cloves

⅛ teaspoon crushed red pepper

4 large garlic cloves, minced

2 (15.5-ounce) cans white hominy, rinsed and drained

2 (4.5-ounce) cans chopped green chiles, undrained

1 cup packaged angel hair slaw

½ cup thinly sliced radishes (4 radishes)

½ cup diced peeled avocado

2 limes, each cut into 4 wedges (optional)

1. Heat a large nonstick skillet over medium high heat. Add oil to pan; swirl to coat. Add pork to pan. Cook 8 minutes, browning on all sides.

2. Combine pork, broth, and next 9 ingredients (through chiles) in a 5-quart electric slow cooker. Cover and cook on LOW for 8 hours. Ladle posole into bowls; top with slaw, radishes, and avocado. Serve with lime wedges, if desired.

CALORIES 213; FAT 6.1g (sat 1.2g, mono 3g, poly 1.3g); PROTEIN 26.7g; CARB 12.4g; FIBER 3.4g; CHOL 74mg; IRON 2.1mg; SODIUM 553mg; CALC 39mg

Thai-Style Pork Stew

Peanut butter melds with traditional Asian ingredients to lend this one-dish meal a Thai flair. Lime makes a perfect accent.

Yield: 8 servings (serving size: 1 cup stew, about ⅔ cup rice, 1 tablespoon green onions, about ½ teaspoon peanuts, and 1 lime wedge)

2 pounds boned pork loin, trimmed and cut into 4 pieces

2 cups (1 x ¼-inch) julienne-cut red bell pepper

¼ cup teriyaki sauce

2 tablespoons rice or white wine vinegar

1 teaspoon crushed red pepper

2 garlic cloves, minced

¼ cup creamy peanut butter

6 cups hot cooked basmati rice

½ cup diagonally cut green onions

2 tablespoons chopped dry-roasted peanuts

8 lime wedges

1. Place pork in an electric slow cooker. Stir in bell pepper and next 4 ingredients (through garlic). Cover and cook on LOW for 8 hours. Remove pork from slow cooker, and coarsely chop. Add peanut butter to liquid in slow cooker; stir well. Stir in pork.

2. Spoon stew over rice. Top each serving with onions and peanuts; serve with lime wedges.

CALORIES 413; FAT 13g (sat 3.6g, mono 5.9g, poly 2.3g); PROTEIN 31.4g; CARB 40.9g; FIBER 2.5g; CHOL 62mg; IRON 2.9mg; SODIUM 456mg; CALC 22mg

Smoky Slow-Cooked Chili

Yield: 8 servings (serving size: about 1⅓ cups chili, 1 tablespoon cilantro, 1 tablespoon green onions, 1 tablespoon cheese, and 1 lime wedge)

1 pound lean ground pork

1 pound boneless pork shoulder (Boston butt), trimmed and cut into ½-inch pieces

3 cups chopped onion

1¾ cups chopped green bell pepper

3 garlic cloves, minced

3 tablespoons tomato paste

1 cup lager-style beer

3 tablespoons chili powder

1 tablespoon ground cumin

2 teaspoons dried oregano

¾ teaspoon freshly ground black pepper

6 tomatillos, quartered

2 bay leaves

2 (14½-ounce) cans plum tomatoes, undrained and chopped

1 (15-ounce) can no-salt-added pinto beans, drained

1 (7¾-ounce) can Mexican-style spicy tomato sauce

1 smoked ham hock (about 8 ounces)

1½ tablespoons sugar

½ cup finely chopped fresh cilantro

½ cup finely chopped green onions

2 ounces crumbled queso fresco (about ½ cup)

8 lime wedges

1. Heat a large nonstick skillet over medium-high heat. Cook ground pork 5 minutes or until browned, stirring to slightly crumble. Drain well. Place pork in an electric slow cooker.

2. Add pork shoulder to pan; cook 5 minutes or until lightly browned, turning occasionally. Transfer pork shoulder to slow cooker.

3. Add onion and bell pepper to pan; cook 8 minutes, stirring frequently. Add garlic; sauté 1 minute. Add tomato paste; cook 1 minute, stirring constantly. Stir in beer; cook 1 minute. Stir onion mixture into mixture in slow cooker. Stir in chili powder and next 9 ingredients (through ham hock). Cover and cook on HIGH for 5 hours or until meat is tender. Remove bay leaves and ham hock; discard. Stir in sugar. Ladle chili into bowls; top each serving with cilantro, green onions, and cheese. Serve with lime wedges.

CALORIES 357; FAT 14.4g (sat 5.2g, mono 5.6g, poly 2g); PROTEIN 27.7g; CARB 27.7g; FIBER 6.8g; CHOL 84mg; IRON 3.4mg; SODIUM 594mg; CALC 113mg

PREP TIP

You can also cook the chili in a slow cooker on LOW for 8 hours. To cook the chili on the cooktop, use 12 ounces of beer and simmer, covered, for 2½ to 3 hours or until the pork shoulder is tender.

Easy Brunswick Stew

Yield: 9 servings (serving size: about 1½ cups)

4 cups frozen Southern-style hash brown potatoes, thawed

2⅓ cups chopped onion

2 cups fat-free, lower-sodium chicken broth

1½ cups frozen lima beans, thawed

1¼ cups chopped green bell pepper

1 cup frozen cut okra, thawed

1 cup barbecue sauce

1 cup chopped cooked chicken breast

½ cup chopped celery

½ teaspoon freshly ground black pepper

¼ teaspoon salt

¾ pound pulled smoked pork, chopped

2 (8-ounce) cans no-salt-added tomato sauce

1 (15¼-ounce) can whole-kernel corn with sweet peppers, drained

1 (14.5-ounce) can no-salt-added diced tomatoes, undrained

1. Combine all ingredients in a 7-quart electric slow cooker. Cover and cook on HIGH for 8 hours.

CALORIES 316; FAT 8.1g (sat 2.9g, mono 3.2g, poly 1.5g); PROTEIN 20.5g; CARB 40.7g; FIBER 5.2g; CHOL 47mg; IRON 2.8mg; SODIUM 649mg; CALC 53mg

FLAVOR TIP

Experiment with different types of barbecue sauce. Each is unique and will lend a slightly different flavor to the stew. Watch out for high-sodium sauces, though. Some sauces are loaded with too much salt.

Smoked Sausage Cassoulet

For a thicker consistency, let the cassoulet stand 30 minutes before serving.

Yield: 8 servings (serving size: 1 cup cassoulet, 1 teaspoon cheese, and 1 teaspoon parsley)

2 bacon slices

2 cups chopped onion

1 teaspoon dried thyme

½ teaspoon dried rosemary

3 garlic cloves, minced

½ teaspoon salt

½ teaspoon freshly ground black pepper

2 (14.5-ounce) cans diced tomatoes, drained

2 (15-ounce) cans Great Northern beans, rinsed and drained

1 pound lean boneless pork loin roast, trimmed and cut into 1-inch cubes

½ pound reduced-fat smoked sausage, cut into ½-inch cubes

8 teaspoons finely shredded fresh Parmesan cheese

8 teaspoons chopped fresh flat-leaf parsley

1. Cook bacon in a large skillet over medium-high heat until crisp. Remove bacon from pan; crumble. Add onion, thyme, rosemary, and garlic to drippings in pan; sauté 3 minutes or until tender. Stir in crumbled bacon, salt, pepper, and tomatoes; bring to a boil. Remove from heat.

2. Place half of beans in a large bowl; mash with a potato masher until chunky. Add remaining half of beans, pork, and sausage; stir well. Place half of bean mixture in a 3½-quart electric slow cooker; top with half of tomato mixture. Repeat layers. Cover and cook on LOW for 5 hours. Ladle into bowls. Sprinkle with Parmesan cheese and parsley.

CALORIES 249; FAT 7.6g (sat 2.7g, mono 3.2g, poly 0.9g); CARB 23.8g; FIBER 4.6g; CHOL 48mg; IRON 2.9mg; SODIUM 627mg; CALC 89mg

Chicken Stew with Green Olives

Yield: 4 servings

2 (14.5-ounce) cans no-salt-added diced tomatoes, drained

1½ cups fat-free, lower-sodium chicken broth, divided

1 onion, sliced

1 garlic clove, minced

1 teaspoon ground cumin

1 teaspoon paprika

½ teaspoon turmeric

1 tablespoon olive oil

1 (3-pound) quartered chicken, skinned

½ teaspoon freshly ground black pepper

⅛ teaspoon kosher salt

½ cup pitted green olives

Grated peel of 1 lemon

2 cups hot cooked couscous

¼ cup sliced almonds, toasted

1. Place tomatoes, 1 cup broth, and next 5 ingredients (through turmeric) in an electric slow cooker.

2. Heat a large skillet over medium high heat. Add oil to pan; swirl to coat. Sprinkle chicken with pepper and salt. Add chicken to pan; cook chicken about 8 minutes, browning on all sides. Place in slow cooker. Pour remaining ½ cup broth into pan, scraping pan to loosen browned bits. Pour liquid into slow cooker.

3. Cover and cook on HIGH for 4 hours. Thirty minutes before end of cooking time, stir in olives and rind.

4. Remove chicken from slow cooker; cool. Remove meat from bones; return meat to slow cooker. Discard bones.

5. Serve stew over couscous, and sprinkle with almonds.

CALORIES 438; FAT 15.6g (sat 2.5g, mono 8.9g, poly 2.7g); PROTEIN 42.4g; CARB 30.5g; FIBER 4.4g; CHOL 113mg; IRON 3.7mg; SODIUM 691mg; CALC 83mg

Spicy Chicken Stew

Salsa and chili powder add spice to this chicken stew, but probably not too much for timid tasters or kids. If you want to kick up the heat, use a hot salsa and a dash of hot sauce or ground red pepper.

Yield: 6 servings

2 baking potatoes (about 1½ pounds), peeled and cut into chunks (3⅓ cups)

1 (10-ounce) package frozen whole-kernel corn

2 celery stalks, chopped

2 carrots, peeled and cut into chunks (1 cup)

1 onion, cut into 1/2-inch-thick slices

2 garlic cloves, minced

1 cup bottled salsa

1½ teaspoons ground cumin

1 teaspoon chili powder

½ teaspoon freshly ground black pepper

1 pound skinless, boneless chicken breast

4 skinless, boneless chicken thighs (about 10.5 ounces)

2½ cups fat-free, lower-sodium chicken broth

4 (6-inch) fresh corn tortillas, cut into strips

Chopped fresh parsley (optional)

1. Place first 6 ingredients in an electric slow cooker. Stir in salsa and next 3 ingredients (through pepper). Place chicken on top of vegetables, and add broth. Cover and cook on HIGH for 4 hours.
2. Remove chicken from slow cooker; shred with 2 forks. Return chicken to slow cooker. Stir tortilla strips into stew. Garnish with parsley, if desired.

CALORIES 403; FAT 4.5g (sat 0.9g, mono 1g, poly 1.4g); PROTEIN 35g; CARB 55.5g; FIBER 4.4g; CHOL 85mg; IRON 2.8mg; SODIUM 643mg; CALC 70mg

Rosemary Chicken Noodle Soup

Add the noodles to the soup just before serving so they don't absorb too much of the broth. To make ahead, cook the soup the night before without adding the noodles, cool to room temperature, and refrigerate. Take the noodles to work in a zip-top plastic bag; add to soup, and then reheat in the microwave or in a slow cooker set on HIGH.

Yield: 10 servings (serving size: 2 cups)

1 tablespoon olive oil, divided

1½ pounds skinless, boneless chicken thighs, cut into 1-inch pieces

1½ pounds skinless, boneless chicken breast, cut into 1-inch pieces

1 teaspoon salt

6 cups water

4 cups fat-free, lower-sodium chicken broth

2 cups chopped onion

1 cup chopped celery

1 tablespoon chopped fresh rosemary

1 (10-ounce) package preshredded carrot

1 (8-ounce) package presliced mushrooms

⅓ cup finely chopped fresh parsley

1 (6-ounce) package fresh baby spinach

¼ cup fresh lemon juice

½ teaspoon freshly ground black pepper

4 cups hot cooked whole-wheat blend wide egg noodles (about 3½ cups uncooked)

1. Heat a large skillet over medium-high heat. Add 1½ teaspoons oil to pan; swirl to coat. Add half of chicken. Cook 3 minutes or until browned, turning once.

2. Place chicken in a 7-quart electric slow cooker. Repeat procedure with remaining oil and chicken.

3. Add salt and next 7 ingredients (through mushrooms) to slow cooker, stirring well. Cover and cook on LOW for 4 hours or until chicken is done. Stir in parsley and next 3 ingredients (through pepper), stirring until spinach wilts. Stir in noodles.

CALORIES 266; FAT 5.4g (sat 1.2g, mono 2.1g, poly 1.1g); PROTEIN 33.6g; CARB 21.2g; FIBER 4.5g; CHOL 96mg; IRON 2.9mg; SODIUM 556mg; CALC 63mg

Tuscan Chicken Soup

This recipe uses many common pantry and refrigerator staples. All you have to pick up at the supermarket is fresh spinach and chicken thighs.

Yield: 4 servings (serving size: 1½ cups soup and 2 teaspoons cheese)

1 cup chopped onion

2 tablespoons tomato paste

¼ teaspoon freshly ground black pepper

⅛ teaspoon salt

1 (15-ounce) can cannellini beans or other white beans, rinsed and drained

1 (14-ounce) can fat-free, lower-sodium chicken broth

1 (7-ounce) bottle roasted red bell peppers, rinsed, drained, and cut into ½-inch pieces

1 pound boneless, skinless chicken thighs, cut into 1-inch pieces

3 garlic cloves, minced

½ teaspoon chopped fresh rosemary

1 (6-ounce) package fresh baby spinach

8 teaspoons grated fresh Parmesan cheese

1. Combine first 9 ingredients in an electric slow cooker. Cover and cook on HIGH for 1 hour. Reduce heat to LOW; cook 3 hours. Stir in rosemary and spinach; cover and cook on LOW for 10 minutes.

2. Ladle soup into bowls; top each serving with cheese.

CALORIES 246; FAT 5.6g (sat 1.8g, mono 1.7g, poly 1.2g); PROTEIN 30g; CARB 18g; FIBER 5.1g; CHOL 97mg; IRON 3.9mg; SODIUM 667mg; CALC 137mg

Peasant Stew

Yield: 6 servings (serving size: 1 chicken thigh, 1¼ cups stew, 2 teaspoons cilantro, and 2 teaspoons sour cream)

1 teaspoon ground cumin

¼ teaspoon salt

¼ teaspoon freshly ground black pepper

6 chicken thighs (about 1½ pounds), skinned

1 cup chopped onion

1 (14.5-ounce) can Mexican-style stewed tomatoes with jalapeño peppers and spices, undrained

1 (4.5-ounce) can chopped green chiles, undrained

1 (15-ounce) can pinto beans, rinsed and drained

1 (15-ounce) can kidney beans, rinsed and drained

¼ cup minced fresh cilantro

¼ cup reduced-fat sour cream

1. Combine cumin, salt, and pepper; sprinkle over chicken.

2. Place chicken in an electric slow cooker; stir in onion, tomatoes, and chiles. Cover and cook on HIGH for 3 hours. Stir in beans. Cover and cook on HIGH for 1 hour.

3. Place chicken thighs in soup bowls; ladle stew into each bowl. Top each serving with cilantro and sour cream.

CALORIES 207; FAT 4.2g (sat 1.4g, mono 1.2g, poly 0.7g); PROTEIN 18.7g; CARB 22.2g; FIBER 6.3g; CHOL 59mg; IRON 2.3mg; SODIUM 674mg; CALC 96mg

Smoked Turkey–Lentil Soup

Throw smoked turkey, dried lentils, and a handful of other ingredients into the slow cooker in the morning, and you'll come home to a comforting meal. If you prefer to use dried oregano instead of the fresh, reduce the amount to ½ teaspoon. Dried herbs are very potent; a little goes a long way.

Yield: 8 servings (serving size: 1 cup)

1 (8-ounce) smoked turkey leg

6 cups organic vegetable broth

½ pound dried lentils, rinsed and drained

1 (8-ounce) container refrigerated prechopped celery, onion, and bell pepper mix

2 teaspoons chopped fresh oregano

½ teaspoon freshly ground black pepper

Plain fat-free Greek yogurt (optional)

Oregano sprigs (optional)

1. Place turkey leg in a 3- to 4-quart electric slow cooker. Stir in broth and next 4 ingredients (through pepper). Cover and cook on LOW for 8 to 10 hours or until lentils are tender and turkey falls off the bone.

2. Remove turkey leg from slow cooker. Remove and discard skin. Shred meat; return to slow cooker, discarding bone. Ladle soup into bowls; garnish with yogurt and oregano sprigs, if desired.

CALORIES 175; FAT 3.5g (sat 0.9g, mono 0.9g, poly 1.1g); PROTEIN 14.6g; CARB 21.3g; FIBER 5g; CHOL 24mg; IRON 2.5mg; SODIUM 704mg; CALC 30mg

Turkey and Hominy Chili

Serve with warm corn bread.

Yield: 8 servings (serving size: 1 cup)

1¼ cups chopped red bell pepper

1 cup chopped onion

1 tablespoon chili powder

1½ teaspoons ground cumin

½ teaspoon dried oregano

⅛ teaspoon salt

6 garlic cloves, minced

1 jalapeño pepper, seeded and minced

1 (2¾-pound) turkey tenderloin

1 (15-ounce) can golden hominy, rinsed and drained

1 (15-ounce) can seasoned diced tomatoes for chili, undrained

1 (14.5-ounce) can no-salt-added diced fire-roasted tomatoes, undrained

4 ounces shredded reduced-fat Colby-Jack cheese (about 1 cup) (optional)

1 cup thinly sliced green onions (optional)

½ cup sliced ripe olives, drained (optional)

1. Combine first 8 ingredients in a 5-quart electric slow cooker.

2. Place turkey on top of vegetables in slow cooker. Add hominy and tomatoes to slow cooker. Cover and cook on LOW for 5½ hours.

3. Remove turkey from slow cooker; cool 10 minutes. Skim solidified fat from surface; discard. Separate turkey into large chunks with 2 forks. Return turkey to slow cooker. Cover and cook on HIGH for 10 minutes or until thoroughly heated.

4. Ladle chili into bowls. Top with cheese, green onions, and olives, if desired.

CALORIES 291; FAT 6.2g (sat 2.6g, mono 1.9g, poly 1g); PROTEIN 44.2g; CARB 16.9g; FIBER 4.1g; CHOL 70mg; IRON 3.3mg; SODIUM 667mg; CALC 247mg

sides
condiments
&desserts

Chunky Applesauce

We left the skins on the McIntosh apples to provide texture and color to this favorite fruit dish.

Yield: 14 servings (serving size: ½ cup)

Cooking spray

4 pounds Golden Delicious apples, peeled and cut into ½-inch slices

2 pounds McIntosh apples, cut into ½-inch slices

½ cup water

¼ cup sugar

6 (3-inch) cinnamon sticks

2 tablespoons fresh lemon juice

¼ cup unsalted butter (optional)

1. Coat a 5-quart electric slow cooker with cooking spray. Combine apples, next 4 ingredients (through juice), and butter, if desired, in slow cooker. Cover and cook on LOW for 6 hours. Stir until desired consistency. Serve warm or chilled.

CALORIES 117; FAT 0.1g; PROTEIN 0.3g; CARB 29.9g; FIBER 4.3g; CHOL 0mg; IRON 6.4mg; SODIUM 0mg; CALC 7mg

INGREDIENT TIP

For chunkier applesauce, do not mash the mixture after cooking.

Santa Fe Black Beans

Yield: 14 servings (serving size: ½ cup beans, about 1 tablespoon cheese, about 1½ teaspoons cilantro, and about 1½ teaspoons pumpkinseed kernels)

1 (1-pound) package dried black beans

3 cups fat-free, lower-sodium chicken broth

2 cups finely chopped onion (about 1 large)

1 tablespoon chopped chipotle chile, canned in adobo sauce

1 teaspoon salt

4 garlic cloves, minced

1 tablespoon fresh lime juice

4 ounces crumbled queso fresco (about 1 cup)

½ cup chopped fresh cilantro

½ cup unsalted pumpkinseed kernels

1. Sort and wash beans; place in a large Dutch oven. Cover with water to 2 inches above beans; bring to a boil. Cook 2 minutes; remove from heat. Cover and let stand 1 hour. Drain beans.

2. Place beans in a 3-quart electric slow cooker. Stir in chicken broth and next 4 ingredients (through garlic). Cover and cook on LOW for 10 hours or until beans are tender.

3. Stir in lime juice. Mash bean mixture with a potato masher until slightly thick. Sprinkle with queso fresco, cilantro, and pumpkinseed kernels.

CALORIES 165; FAT 4.4g (sat 1.8g, mono 1.2g, poly 0.9g); PROTEIN 9.8g; CARB 23.1g; FIBER 3.5g; CHOL 6mg; IRON 2mg; SODIUM 347mg; CALC 9mg

Southern-Style Green Beans

Infused with deep bacon and onion flavor, these tender beans are just like your grandmother used to make. Serve with pepper sauce for an extra kick, if desired.

Yield: 8 servings (serving size: ½ cup beans and 1½ teaspoons bacon)

3 center-cut bacon slices

1 cup chopped onion

1 cup fat-free, lower-sodium chicken broth

¼ teaspoon salt

1½ pounds green beans, trimmed

Hot pepper sauce (optional)

1. Cook bacon in a large nonstick skillet over medium heat 6 minutes or until crisp. Remove bacon from pan, reserving 1 teaspoon drippings in pan; crumble bacon. Add onion to drippings in pan; sauté 5 minutes or until tender.

2. Combine onion, broth, salt, and green beans in a 4-quart electric slow cooker. Cover and cook on LOW for 8 hours or until beans are very tender. Transfer beans from slow cooker to a serving bowl, using a slotted spoon. Sprinkle with crumbled bacon. Serve with hot pepper sauce, if desired.

CALORIES 38; FAT 0.8g (sat 0.4g, mono 0.6g, poly 0.1g); PROTEIN 2.1g; CARB 7g; FIBER 3.4g; CHOL 3mg; IRON 0.4mg; SODIUM 181mg; CALC 46mg

Honey-Orange Carrots

Brighten up any weeknight meal with this healthy side dish loaded with vitamins. (Pictured on page 224)

Yield: 13 servings (serving size: ½ cup)

3 pounds carrots, diagonally cut into 3-inch pieces

2 tablespoons water

½ cup honey

½ teaspoon salt

2 tablespoons butter, cut into pieces

½ teaspoon grated orange rind

1. Place carrots, 2 tablespoons water, and honey in a 4-quart electric slow cooker.

2. Sprinkle salt over carrots. Sprinkle butter pieces over mixture. Cover and cook on LOW for 8 hours or until carrots are very tender. Transfer carrots to a bowl; stir in orange rind.

CALORIES 98; FAT 2g (sat 1.2g, mono 0.5g, poly 0.2g); PROTEIN 1.1g; CARB 20.5g; FIBER 2.9g; CHOL 5mg; IRON 0.4mg; SODIUM 176mg; CALC 36mg

QUICK TIP

Use a Microplane grater to quickly grate the orange rind.

Lemon-Rosemary Beets

A little lemon juice brings out the vivid color in these beets and keeps the flavors bright, too.

Yield: 7 servings (serving size: ½ cup)

2 pounds beets (about 6), peeled and cut into wedges

2 tablespoons fresh lemon juice

2 tablespoons extra-virgin olive oil

2 tablespoons honey

1 tablespoon cider vinegar

¾ teaspoon kosher salt

½ teaspoon freshly ground black pepper

2 rosemary sprigs

½ teaspoon grated lemon rind

1. Place first 8 ingredients in a 4-quart electric slow cooker. Cover and cook on LOW for 8 hours or until beets are tender. Remove and discard rosemary sprigs; stir in lemon rind.

CALORIES 112; FAT 4.2g (sat 0.6g, mono 3.1g, poly 0.4g); PROTEIN 2.2g; CARB 17.8g; FIBER 3.7g; CHOL 0mg; IRON 1.2mg; SODIUM 239mg; CALC 22mg

Balsamic Collard Greens

Serve these greens with pork tenderloin and garlic mashed potatoes.

Yield: 5 servings (serving size: ½ cup collard greens and 2½ teaspoons bacon)

3 bacon slices

1 cup chopped onion

1 (16-ounce) package chopped fresh collard greens

¼ teaspoon salt

2 garlic cloves, minced

1 bay leaf

1 (14.5-ounce) can fat-free, lower-sodium chicken broth

3 tablespoons balsamic vinegar

1 tablespoon honey

1. Cook bacon in a large Dutch oven over medium heat until crisp. Remove bacon from pan; crumble. Add onion to drippings in pan; sauté 5 minutes or until tender. Add collard greens, and cook 2 to 3 minutes or until greens begin to wilt, stirring occasionally.

2. Place collard green mixture, salt, and next 3 ingredients (through broth) in a 3-quart electric slow cooker. Cover and cook on LOW for 3½ to 4 hours.

3. Combine balsamic vinegar and honey in a small bowl. Stir vinegar mixture into collard greens just before serving. Sprinkle with bacon.

CALORIES 82; FAT 1.8g (sat 0.8g, mono 0.8g, poly 0.4g); PROTEIN 5g; CARB 13.6g; FIBER 3.8g; CHOL 6mg; IRON 0.3mg; SODIUM 260mg; CALC 144mg

Poblano Corn Pudding

Guaranteed to heat up any meal, this corn pudding is a tasty menu item for a Mexican-themed buffet.

Yield: 8 servings (serving size: ½ cup)

4 large poblano chiles (10 ounces)

Cooking spray

½ cup 1% low-fat milk

¼ cup yellow cornmeal

1.1 ounces all-purpose flour (about ¼ cup)

2 tablespoons sugar

2 tablespoons butter, melted

1 teaspoon baking powder

¼ teaspoon salt

2 large eggs, lightly beaten

1 (8¼-ounce) can cream-style corn

2 cups frozen whole-kernel corn

4 ounces reduced-fat cheddar cheese with jalapeño peppers, shredded (about 1 cup)

1. Preheat broiler.

2. Place poblano chiles on a foil-lined baking sheet. Broil 8 minutes or until blackened and charred, turning after 6 minutes. Place in a paper bag; fold to close tightly. Let stand 15 minutes. Peel and discard skins. Discard seeds and stems. Chop chiles.

3. Coat an oval 3-quart electric slow cooker with cooking spray. Place milk and next 7 ingredients (through eggs) in slow cooker; stir with a whisk until blended. Stir in chiles, corn, and cheese. Cover and cook on LOW for 2½ hours or until set. Remove lid. Cook on LOW for 15 minutes.

CALORIES 183; FAT 5.8g (sat 2.9g, mono 1.6g, poly 0.5g); PROTEIN 9.1g; CARB 26.5g; FIBER 1.7g; CHOL 65mg; IRON 1.1mg; SODIUM 353mg; CALC 185mg

Spicy Black-Eyed Peas

Yield: 7 servings (serving size: ½ cup)

3 cups shelled black-eyed peas

2 cups fat-free, lower-sodium chicken broth

2 cups chopped sweet onion

2 tablespoons finely chopped jalapeño pepper

½ teaspoon dried thyme

¼ teaspoon salt

¼ teaspoon freshly ground black pepper

4 garlic cloves, minced

1 (12-ounce) smoked turkey leg

1 bay leaf

Hot sauce (optional)

1. Place all ingredients except hot sauce in a 3-quart electric slow cooker; stir well. Cover and cook on LOW for 8 hours or until peas are tender. Discard bay leaf and turkey leg. Serve peas with a slotted spoon, and sprinkle with hot sauce, if desired.

CALORIES 135; FAT 2.8g (sat 1g, mono 0.7g, poly 0.8g); PROTEIN 10.4g; CARB 17g; FIBER 4g; CHOL 22mg; IRON 1.5mg; SODIUM 287mg; CALC 101mg

FREEZER TIP

Freeze your summer bounty of black-eyed peas for fresh flavor in the fall. Fill a heavy-duty zip-top plastic bag with unrinsed peas, and place in the freezer. Use within three months for best taste.

Loaded Twice-Baked Potatoes

For a main dish, split the potatoes from the top, and open slightly; pile on more toppings, and enjoy the entire potato.

Yield: 8 servings (serving size: 1 potato half)

4 small baking potatoes (about 6 ounces each)

Cooking spray

⅛ teaspoon kosher salt

¼ cup fat-free milk

¼ cup plain fat-free Greek yogurt

2 ounces shredded reduced-fat sharp cheddar cheese (about ½ cup), divided

¼ teaspoon kosher salt

¼ teaspoon freshly ground black pepper

1 tablespoon chopped fresh chives

2 bacon slices, cooked and crumbled

1. Scrub potatoes; rinse and pat dry with paper towels. Coat potatoes with cooking spray; pierce potatoes with a fork. Rub ⅛ teaspoon kosher salt evenly over potatoes; place in an oval 6-quart electric slow cooker. Cover and cook on LOW for 8 hours or until potatoes are tender. Cool slightly.

2. Cut each potato in half lengthwise; scoop out pulp into a medium microwave-safe bowl, leaving a ⅛-inch-thick shell. Mash pulp with a potato masher. Stir in milk, yogurt, ¼ cup cheese, ¼ teaspoon kosher salt, and pepper. Microwave at HIGH 1 minute or until thoroughly heated.

3. Spoon potato mixture evenly into shells; sprinkle evenly with remaining ¼ cup cheese. Arrange potato halves in bottom of slow cooker. Cover and cook on HIGH for 25 minutes or until thoroughly heated and cheese melts. Sprinkle each potato half with about ½ teaspoon chives and about 1 teaspoon bacon.

CALORIES 194; FAT 12.7g (sat 1.2g, mono 0.6g, poly 0.1g); PROTEIN 4.9g; CARB 15.8g; FIBER 1.9g; CHOL 7mg; IRON 1mg; SODIUM 193mg; CALC 126mg

Sweet Potato Gratin

A sprinkle of Parmesan and thyme adds a unique twist to this savory sweet potato gratin.

Yield: 12 servings (serving size: ½ cup)

1 tablespoon butter, softened

1 cup thinly sliced sweet onion

2 pounds sweet potatoes (about 3 large), peeled and thinly sliced

1 tablespoon all-purpose flour

1 teaspoon chopped fresh thyme

½ teaspoon kosher salt

½ teaspoon freshly ground black pepper

2 ounces grated fresh Parmesan cheese (about ½ cup), divided

Cooking spray

½ cup organic vegetable broth

1. Melt butter in a medium nonstick skillet over medium heat. Add onion; sauté 5 minutes or until lightly browned. Combine onion, sweet potato, next 4 ingredients (through pepper), and ¼ cup cheese in a large bowl, tossing to coat with flour. Coat a 4-quart electric slow cooker with cooking spray. Transfer vegetable mixture to slow cooker.

2. Pour broth over potato mixture. Sprinkle with remaining ¼ cup cheese. Cover and cook on LOW for 4 hours or until potato is tender.

CALORIES 90; FAT 2.5g (sat 1.3g, mono 0.6g, poly 0.1g); PROTEIN 3.4g; CARB 13.8g; FIBER 2.2g; CHOL 6mg; IRON 1mg; SODIUM 216mg; CALC 93mg

Orange-Fig Jam

Serve this honey-colored jam alongside goat cheese or ⅓-less-fat cream cheese with assorted crackers. The recipe makes a lot, so store in decorative jars in your refrigerator to serve to unexpected guests and at impromptu parties. Tie on a pretty ribbon to present as a hostess gift.

Yield: 64 servings (serving size: 1 tablespoon)

1¾ cups water

1½ cups sugar

¼ cup Grand Marnier (orange-flavored liqueur)

¼ cup fresh orange juice

2 (7-ounce) packages dried Calimyrna figs, coarsely chopped

1 teaspoon grated orange rind

1. Place all ingredients except orange rind in a 2½-quart electric slow cooker; stir until sugar dissolves. Cover and cook on LOW for 6 hours. Stir in orange rind.
2. Place half of fig mixture in a food processor; process until smooth. Pour into a bowl. Repeat procedure with remaining fig mixture. Ladle jam into hot sterilized jars. Cover jars with metal lids; screw on bands. Cool to room temperature. Chill thoroughly; store in refrigerator.

CALORIES 37; FAT 0.1g; PROTEIN 0.2g; CARB 9g; FIBER 0.6g; CHOL 0mg; IRON 0.1mg; SODIUM 1mg; CALC 10mg

Overnight Apple Butter

Make a sweet, rich apple butter spread that is perfect slathered on a toasted English muffin or served over pork chops. One taste, and you'll never believe it's fat free.

Yield: 4 cups (serving size: ¼ cup)

1 cup packed brown sugar

½ cup honey

¼ cup apple cider

1 tablespoon ground cinnamon

¼ teaspoon ground cloves

⅛ teaspoon ground mace

10 medium apples, peeled and cut into large chunks (about 2½ pounds)

1. Place all ingredients in a 5-quart electric slow cooker; stir well. Cover and cook on LOW for 10 hours or until apples are very tender.
2. Place a large sieve over a bowl; spoon one-third of apple mixture into sieve. Press mixture through sieve using the back of a spoon or ladle. Discard pulp. Repeat procedure with remaining apple mixture. Return apple mixture to slow cooker. Increase heat to HIGH. Cook, uncovered, on HIGH for 1½ hours or until mixture is thick, stirring occasionally. Spoon into a bowl; cover and chill for up to a week.

CALORIES 132; FAT 0g; PROTEIN 0.1g; CARB 35.3g; FIBER 3.1g; CHOL 0mg; IRON 0.7mg; SODIUM 6mg; CALC 18mg

Chunky Peach-Ginger Chutney

If you use frozen peaches, there's no need to thaw them first. This chutney thickens as it stands, as well as when it chills. Serve the chutney warm or chilled with grilled or roasted pork, chicken, or lamb.

Yield: 4¼ cups (serving size: ¼ cup)

2 cups chopped onion

4 cups fresh or frozen sliced peeled peaches

1 cup golden raisins

1 cup firmly packed light brown sugar

¼ cup crystallized ginger

1 teaspoon mustard seeds

½ teaspoon ground ginger

¼ teaspoon ground cinnamon

¼ teaspoon ground cloves

1.1 ounces all-purpose flour (about ¼ cup)

¼ cup cider vinegar

1. Place a large nonstick skillet over medium-high heat. Add chopped onion, and sauté 5 minutes or until tender.
2. Place onion, peaches, and next 7 ingredients (through cloves) in a 3-quart electric slow cooker; stir well. Weigh or lightly spoon flour into a dry measuring cup; level with a knife. Combine flour and vinegar in a small bowl; stir with a whisk until well blended. Add flour mixture to peach mixture; stir well. Cover and cook on LOW for 5 hours.

CALORIES 120; FAT 0.2g (sat 0g, mono 0.1g, poly 0.1g); PROTEIN 1g; CARB 29.3g; FIBER 1.4g; CHOL 0mg; IRON 1mg; SODIUM 8mg; CALC 28mg

Tiramisu Bread Pudding

Drizzled with a rich mascarpone sauce, this moist, coffee- and Kahlúa-flavored bread pudding offers the flavors of a favorite Italian dessert.

Yield: 10 servings (serving size: ½ cup pudding, about 1 tablespoon sauce, and about ¼ teaspoon cocoa)

½ cup water

⅓ cup sugar

1½ tablespoons instant espresso granules

2 tablespoons Kahlúa (coffee-flavored liqueur)

2 cups 1% low-fat milk, divided

2 large eggs, lightly beaten

8 cups (1-inch) cubed French bread (about 8 ounces)

Cooking spray

⅓ cup mascarpone cheese

1 teaspoon vanilla extract

2 teaspoons unsweetened cocoa

1. Combine first 3 ingredients in a small saucepan. Bring to a boil; boil 1 minute, stirring occasionally. Remove from heat; stir in liqueur.
2. Combine 1¾ cups milk and eggs in a large bowl, stirring with a whisk. Add espresso mixture, stirring with whisk. Add bread, stirring to coat. Pour bread mixture into a 2½-quart round casserole coated with cooking spray. Place dish in an oval 7-quart electric slow cooker. Cover and cook on LOW for 2 hours or until set.
3. Combine remaining ¼ cup milk, mascarpone cheese, and vanilla in a small bowl, stirring with a whisk until smooth. Spoon bread pudding into dessert dishes; top each with mascarpone sauce, and sprinkle with cocoa.

CALORIES 199; FAT 9g (sat 4.5g, mono 1.9g, poly 0.4g); PROTEIN 6.7g; CARB 23.5g; FIBER 0.7g; CHOL 63mg; IRON 1.1mg; SODIUM 191mg; CALC 95mg

Spiced Poached Pears

Yield: 6 servings (serving size: 2 pear halves and about 3 tablespoons sauce)

6 firm ripe Anjou pears (2¾ pounds), peeled

1 (500-milliliter) bottle Vino Santo or other sweet dessert wine

½ cup sugar

⅓ cup fresh orange juice

1 (3-inch) vanilla bean, split lengthwise

¼ teaspoon juniper berries

1 (3-inch) cinnamon stick

6 tablespoons crème fraîche (optional)

Ground cinnamon (optional)

1. Remove cores from blossom ends of pears, leaving stem end intact. If necessary, cut about ¼ inch from base of each pear so it sits flat. Place wine, sugar, and orange juice in an oval 5-quart electric slow cooker; stir until sugar dissolves. Scrape seeds from vanilla bean; stir seeds and bean into wine mixture. Add juniper berries and cinnamon stick. Set pears in wine mixture. Cover and cook on HIGH for 3 hours or until pears are tender.

2. Remove pears from cooking liquid. Cut pears in half. Place pear halves in dessert dishes.

3. Pour cooking liquid into a sieve over a medium saucepan; discard solids. Bring to a boil; boil 20 minutes or until reduced to 1 cup. Drizzle sauce evenly over pears. Top with crème fraîche and sprinkle with cinnamon, if desired.

CALORIES 257; FAT 0.2g (sat 0g, mono 0.1g, poly 0.1g); PROTEIN 0.9g; CARB 53g; FIBER 6.2g; CHOL 0mg; IRON 2.8mg; SODIUM 7mg; CALC 23mg

Brandied Plum–Vanilla Bread Pudding

Brandy-spiked dried plums bejewel this delicious vanilla-infused bread pudding, putting a decadent spin on comfort.

Yield: 8 servings (serving size: ⅔ cup)

¾ cup pitted dried plums, quartered

⅓ cup brandy

1½ cups 2% reduced-fat milk

½ cup sugar

1 tablespoon vanilla extract

⅛ teaspoon salt

3 large eggs

5 cups (½-inch) cubed dry French bread (6 ounces)

Cooking spray

½ cup vanilla light ice cream (optional)

1. Place plums and brandy in a bowl. Let stand 30 minutes. Pour mixture into a sieve over a bowl, reserving soaking liquid. Set plums aside.

2. Combine reserved soaking liquid, milk, and next 4 ingredients (through eggs) in a large bowl, stirring well with a whisk. Add bread, tossing gently to coat. Stir in plums. Spoon mixture into a 1½-quart round casserole coated with cooking spray. (Dish will be full.) Cover with foil; let rest 30 minutes to absorb liquid. Remove foil.

3. Place dish in a 5-quart round electric slow cooker; add enough hot water to cooker to come halfway up sides of dish. Place several layers of paper towels across top of slow cooker. Cover and cook on LOW for 4 hours or until a wooden pick inserted in center comes out clean.

4. Remove dish from slow cooker. Serve bread pudding warm. Top with ice cream, if desired.

CALORIES 212; FAT 3.3g (sat 1.3g, mono 1g, poly 0.5g); PROTEIN 6.7g; CARB 33.9g; FIBER 1.4g; CHOL 83mg; IRON 1.2mg; SODIUM 222mg; CALC 79mg

Vanilla Bean Baked Custard

Using evaporated milk helps the custard stabilize and not curdle.

Yield: 4 servings (serving size: 1 custard)

1 (12-ounce) can evaporated low-fat milk

½ cup 1% low-fat milk

1 teaspoon vanilla bean paste

1 large egg, lightly beaten

2 large egg yolks

⅓ cup sugar

1. Combine milks in a medium saucepan. Bring to a simmer over medium heat, about 4 minutes. Remove from heat; add vanilla bean paste, stirring with a whisk until blended.
2. Combine egg, egg yolks, and sugar in a medium bowl, stirring with a whisk until blended. Gradually add hot milk, stirring vigorously with a whisk. Pour egg mixture through a sieve into a bowl.
3. Place 4 metal canning jar bands in bottom of a 6-quart oval electric slow cooker. Ladle egg mixture evenly into 4 (8-ounce) ramekins. Cover ramekins with foil. Set 1 ramekin on each band, making sure ramekins do not touch each other or sides of slow cooker. Carefully pour hot water into slow cooker to depth of 1 inch up sides of ramekins.
4. Cover and cook on HIGH for 1 hour and 45 minutes or until a knife inserted in center of custards comes out clean. Remove ramekins from slow cooker, and cool on a wire rack. Serve warm or chilled.

CALORIES 193; FAT 5.2g (sat 2.7g, mono 1.6g, poly 0.6g); PROTEIN 9.3g; CARB 27.4g; FIBER 0g; CHOL 173mg; IRON 0.5mg; SODIUM 130mg; CALC 269mg

Pineapple-Coconut Tapioca

Small pearl tapioca combined with coconut milk and fresh pineapple makes a simple tropics-inspired treat. The key to success is using small pearl tapioca, not instant or minute tapioca. Fresh mango or papaya works equally well as a substitute for the fresh pineapple.

Yield: 9 servings (serving size: ½ cup tapioca and about 1 tablespoon coconut)

Cooking spray

¾ cup sugar

½ cup regular small pearl tapioca

2 (13.5-ounce) cans light coconut milk

1 large egg

½ cup finely chopped fresh pineapple

½ cup flaked sweetened coconut, toasted

1. Coat a 4-quart electric slow cooker with cooking spray. Combine sugar, tapioca, and coconut milk in slow cooker, stirring with a whisk. Cover and cook on LOW for 2 hours or until most of tapioca is transparent. (Pudding will be thin.)

2. Place egg in a medium bowl; stir with a whisk. Add ½ cup hot tapioca mixture to egg, stirring constantly with a whisk. Stir egg mixture into remaining tapioca mixture in slow cooker. Cover and cook on LOW for 30 minutes. Turn off slow cooker. Stir pineapple into tapioca mixture; cover and let stand 30 minutes. Serve warm or chilled. Top each serving with toasted coconut.

CALORIES 141; FAT 3g (sat 2.3g, mono 0.3g, poly 0.1g); PROTEIN 1.1g; CARB 28.4g; FIBER 0.7g; CHOL 24mg; IRON 0.3mg; SODIUM 25mg; CALC 7mg

Angel Food Cake with Mixed Berry Compote

Slow-cooked sauce made from three types of berries dresses up store-bought pound cake.

Yield: 8 servings (serving size: 1 cake slice and about ⅔ cup berry compote)

Cooking spray

2 cups blueberries

2 cups blackberries

2 cups raspberries

1 cup orange juice

½ cup sugar

3 tablespoons cornstarch

6 tablespoons water

1 (8-ounce) angel food cake, cut into 8 slices

1. Coat a 5-quart electric slow cooker with cooking spray. Combine berries, orange juice, and sugar in slow cooker. Cover and cook on HIGH for 2 hours.

2. Combine cornstarch and water in a small bowl, stirring until smooth. Stir cornstarch mixture into berry mixture. Cover and cook on HIGH for 15 minutes or until sauce thickens. Serve compote over angel food cake.

CALORIES 201; FAT 0.9g (sat 0.1g, mono 0.1g, poly 0.4g); PROTEIN 3g; CARB 47.4g; FIBER 5.2g; CHOL 0mg; IRON 0.8mg; SODIUM 214mg; CALC 64mg

INGREDIENT TIP

If you only have one or two types of berries, you can still make this compote. Just make sure the berries add up to a total of 6 cups.

Amaretti Cheesecake

To prevent the pan from touching the bottom of the slow cooker, you'll need a small rack that fits inside your cooker. If you don't have one, make a ring out of aluminum foil.

Yield: 10 servings (serving size: 1 wedge)

Crust:

⅔ cup amaretti cookie crumbs (about 16 cookies)

2 tablespoons butter, melted

1 tablespoon sugar

Cooking spray

Filling:

2 (8-ounce) blocks fat-free cream cheese, softened and divided

1 (8-ounce) block ⅓-less-fat cream cheese, softened

⅔ cup sugar

1 tablespoon all-purpose flour

2 large eggs

¾ teaspoon almond extract

Raspberries (optional)

1. To prepare crust, combine first 3 ingredients, tossing with a fork until moist and crumbly. Gently press mixture into bottom of a 7-inch springform pan coated with cooking spray.

2. To prepare filling, beat 1 block fat-free cream cheese and ⅓-less-fat cream cheese with a mixer at medium speed until smooth. Add remaining 1 block fat-free cream cheese; beat until blended. Add ⅔ cup sugar and flour; beat well. Add eggs, 1 at a time, beating well after each addition. Stir in almond extract. Pour batter over crust in pan.

3. Pour 1 cup hot water into bottom of a 5-quart electric slow cooker. Place a rack in slow cooker (rack should be taller than water level). Place pan on rack. Place several layers of paper towels over slow cooker insert. Cover and cook on HIGH for 2 hours or until center of cheesecake barely moves when pan is touched. Remove lid from slow cooker; turn off heat, and run a knife around outside edge. Let cheesecake stand in slow cooker 1 hour. Remove cheesecake from slow cooker. Cool to room temperature in pan on a wire rack. Cover and chill at least 6 hours. Cut into wedges. Garnish with raspberries, if desired.

CALORIES 232; FAT 24.3g (sat 5.3g, mono 2.6g, poly 0.9g); PROTEIN 11.2g; CARB 31.7g; FIBER 0.4g; CHOL 120mg; IRON 0.5mg; SODIUM 390mg; CALC 168mg

Rum-Raisin Arborio Pudding

Soaking the raisins in rum allows them to absorb the flavor and plump up before you stir them into the pudding.

Yield: 6 servings (serving size: about ½ cup)

½ cup raisins

¼ cup dark rum

1 (12-ounce) can evaporated low-fat milk

1½ cups water

⅓ cup sugar

¾ cup Arborio rice

¼ teaspoon salt

¼ teaspoon freshly grated nutmeg

1. Combine raisins and rum. Cover and set aside.

2. Combine evaporated milk and 1½ cups water in a medium saucepan. Bring to a simmer over medium heat. Add sugar, stirring to dissolve. Remove from heat.

3. Pour milk mixture into a 3-quart electric slow cooker. Stir in rice and salt. Cover and cook on LOW for 4 hours or just until pudding is set in center, stirring after 1 hour and again after 3 hours.

4. Stir in raisin mixture and nutmeg; let stand, uncovered, 10 minutes. Serve warm.

CALORIES 232; FAT 1.2g (sat 0.9g, mono 0g, poly 0g); PROTEIN 5.9g; CARB 45.1g; FIBER 1.8g; CHOL 9mg; IRON 0.4mg; SODIUM 167mg; CALC 147mg

Brownie Pudding Cake

Rich and decadent from both Dutch process cocoa and bittersweet chocolate, this dessert is part cake and part pudding. Top with vanilla light ice cream, if desired.

Yield: 8 servings (serving size: ⅛ of cake)

4.5 ounces all-purpose flour (about 1 cup)

1¼ cups sugar

¼ cup Dutch process cocoa

¼ teaspoon salt

¼ cup canola oil

1 teaspoon vanilla extract

3 large egg whites

2 large eggs

2 ounces bittersweet chocolate, melted

¼ cup coarsely chopped walnuts, toasted

Cooking spray

1 teaspoon powdered sugar (optional)

1. Weigh or lightly spoon flour into a dry measuring cup; level with a knife. Combine flour, sugar, cocoa, and salt, stirring with a whisk.

2. Combine canola oil and next 3 ingredients (through eggs), stirring with a whisk. Add to dry ingredients, stirring until blended. Stir in melted chocolate. Stir in walnuts.

3. Coat a 3-quart electric slow cooker with cooking spray. Pour batter into slow cooker. Cover and cook on LOW for 2 to 2½ hours or until set around edges but still soft in the center. Turn off slow cooker. Let stand, covered, 30 minutes before serving. Sprinkle with powdered sugar, if desired.

CALORIES 324; FAT 14.6g (sat 2.7g, mono 5.5g, poly 3.9g); PROTEIN 5.2g; CARB 48.7g; FIBER 1.4g; CHOL 30mg; IRON 1.6mg; SODIUM 105mg; CALC 11mg

Double Apple Cake

Yield: 8 servings (serving size: 1 wedge)

Cooking spray

6.75 ounces all-purpose flour (about 1½ cups)

⅓ cup packed dark brown sugar

1 teaspoon baking soda

1½ teaspoons ground cinnamon

½ teaspoon baking powder

¼ teaspoon salt

¼ teaspoon ground nutmeg

⅛ teaspoon ground cloves

1 cup unsweetened applesauce

⅓ cup low-fat buttermilk

¼ cup butter, melted

1 tablespoon vanilla extract

1 large egg

1 cup dried apple slices, coarsely chopped

1 teaspoon powdered sugar (optional)

1. Coat a 5-quart round electric slow cooker with cooking spray. Line bottom of slow cooker with parchment paper. Place 2 (30-inch-long) strips of parchment paper in an X pattern under parchment paper liner in slow cooker. Coat parchment with cooking spray.

2. Weigh or lightly spoon flour into dry measuring cups; level with a knife. Combine flour, brown sugar, and next 6 ingredients (through cloves) in a medium bowl, stirring with a whisk. Combine applesauce and next 4 ingredients (through egg) in a small bowl. Add applesauce mixture to flour mixture, stirring until smooth. Stir in dried apple.

3. Pour batter into prepared slow cooker, spreading into an even layer. Cover and cook on HIGH for 1 to 1½ hours or until puffed and a wooden pick inserted into center comes out clean. Cut into wedges. Sprinkle with powdered sugar, if desired.

CALORIES 235; FAT 6.9g (sat 4g, mono 1.8g, poly 0.4g); PROTEIN 4g; CARB 39.2g; FIBER 1.8g; CHOL 42mg; IRON 1.5mg; SODIUM 354mg; CALC 52mg

Tropical Bananas Foster

Peel and slice the bananas just before adding them to the slow cooker.

Yield: 7 servings (serving size: about ½ cup banana mixture and ¼ cup ice cream)

Cooking spray

½ cup packed dark brown sugar

3 tablespoons butter

¼ cup light coconut milk

¼ cup dark rum

1 cup (1-inch) cubed fresh pineapple

¼ teaspoon ground cinnamon

4 ripe bananas, cut into ½-inch-thick slices

1¾ cups vanilla light ice cream

1. Coat a 3-quart electric slow cooker with cooking spray. Combine brown sugar and next 3 ingredients (through rum) in slow cooker. Cover and cook on LOW for 1 hour. Stir with a whisk until smooth.
2. Add pineapple, cinnamon, and banana to sauce, stirring to coat. Cover and cook on LOW for 15 minutes. Serve immediately over ice cream.

CALORIES 307; FAT 12.2g (sat 5.5g, mono 2.2g, poly 0.4g); PROTEIN 3g; CARB 44g; FIBER 2.1g; CHOL 42mg; IRON 0.6mg; SODIUM 96mg; CALC 98mg

QUICK TIP

Fresh pineapple is a treat, but sometimes for the sake of convenience, the precut variety is worth reaching for. Either way, you can't go wrong.

Walnut-Stuffed Apples

Serve these apples warm from the slow cooker with vanilla light ice cream.

Yield: 4 servings (serving size: 1 apple and ¼ cup cooking liquid)

¼ cup coarsely chopped walnuts

3 tablespoons dried currants

2½ tablespoons brown sugar

¾ teaspoon ground cinnamon, divided

4 medium Granny Smith apples, cored

1 cup packed brown sugar

¾ cup apple cider

1. Combine first 3 ingredients in a small bowl; add ¼ teaspoon cinnamon, stirring to combine. Peel top third of each apple; place apples in an electric slow cooker. Spoon walnut mixture into cavity of each apple.

2. Combine remaining ½ teaspoon cinnamon, 1 cup brown sugar, and apple cider in a small bowl, stirring to combine. Pour over apples. Cover and cook on LOW for 2 hours and 45 minutes. Remove apples from slow cooker with a slotted spoon. Spoon cooking liquid over each serving.

CALORIES 310; FAT 4.9g (sat 0.5g, mono 0.7g, poly 3.6g); PROTEIN 1.9g; CARB 70g; FIBER 3.8g; CHOL 0mg; IRON 1.6mg; SODIUM 23mg; CALC 60mg

Nutritional Analysis

How to Use It and Why

Glance at the end of any *Cooking Light* recipe, and you'll see how committed we are to helping you make the best of today's light cooking. With chefs, registered dietitians, home economists, and a computer system that analyzes every ingredient we use, *Cooking Light* gives you authoritative dietary detail like no other magazine. We go to such lengths so you can see how our recipes fit into your healthful eating plan. If you're trying to lose weight, the calorie and fat figures will probably help most. But if you're keeping a close eye on the sodium, cholesterol, and saturated fat in your diet, we provide those numbers, too. And because many women don't get enough iron or calcium, we can help there, as well. Finally, there's a fiber analysis for those of us who don't get enough roughage.

Here's a helpful guide to put our nutritional analysis numbers into perspective. Remember, one size doesn't fit all, so take your lifestyle, age, and circumstances into consideration when determining your nutrition needs. For example, pregnant or breast-feeding women need more protein, calories, and calcium. And women older than 50 need 1,200mg of calcium daily, 200mg more than the amount recommended for younger women and men.

In Our Nutritional Analysis, We Use These Abbreviations

sat	saturated fat	**CHOL**	cholesterol
mono	monounsaturated fat	**CALC**	calcium
poly	polyunsaturated fat	**g**	gram
CARB	carbohydrates	**mg**	milligram

Daily Nutrition Guide

	Women ages 25 to 50	Women over 50	Men ages 24 to 50	Men over 50
Calories	2,000	2,000 or less	2,700	2,500
Protein	50g	50g or less	63g	60g
Fat	65g or less	65g or less	88g or less	83g or less
Saturated Fat	20g or less	20g or less	27g or less	25g or less
Carbohydrates	304g	304g	410g	375g
Fiber	25g to 35g	25g to 35g	25g to 35g	25g to 35g
Cholesterol	300mg or less	300mg or less	300mg or less	300mg or less
Iron	18mg	8mg	8mg	8mg
Sodium	2,300mg or less	1,500mg or less	2,300mg or less	1,500mg or less
Calcium	1,000mg	1,200mg	1,000mg	1,000mg

The nutritional values used in our calculations either come from The Food Processor, Version 8.9 (ESHA Research), or are provided by food manufacturers.

Metric Equivalents

The information in the following charts is provided to help cooks outside the United States successfully use the recipes in this book. All equivalents are approximate.

Cooking/Oven Temperatures

	Fahrenheit	Celsius	Gas Mark
Freeze Water	32° F	0° C	
Room Temp.	68° F	20° C	
Boil Water	212° F	100° C	
Bake	325° F	160° C	3
	350° F	180° C	4
	375° F	190° C	5
	400° F	200° C	6
	425° F	220° C	7
	450° F	230° C	8
Broil			Grill

Liquid Ingredients by Volume

¼ tsp	=					1 ml		
½ tsp	=					2 ml		
1 tsp	=					5 ml		
3 tsp	=	1 tbl	=	½ fl oz	=	15 ml		
2 tbls	=	⅛ cup	=	1 fl oz	=	30 ml		
4 tbls	=	¼ cup	=	2 fl oz	=	60 ml		
5⅓ tbls	=	⅓ cup	=	3 fl oz	=	80 ml		
8 tbls	=	½ cup	=	4 fl oz	=	120 ml		
10⅔ tbls	=	⅔ cup	=	5 fl oz	=	160 ml		
12 tbls	=	¾ cup	=	6 fl oz	=	180 ml		
16 tbls	=	1 cup	=	8 fl oz	=	240 ml		
1 pt	=	2 cups	=	16 fl oz	=	480 ml		
1 qt	=	4 cups	=	32 fl oz	=	960 ml		
				33 fl oz	=	1000 ml	=	1 l

Dry Ingredients by Weight

(To convert ounces to grams, multiply the number of ounces by 30.)

1 oz	=	¹⁄₁₆ lb	=	30 g
4 oz	=	¼ lb	=	120 g
8 oz	=	½ lb	=	240 g
12 oz	=	¾ lb	=	360 g
16 oz	=	1 lb	=	480 g

Length

(To convert inches to centimeters, multiply the number of inches by 2.5.)

1 in	=				2.5 cm	
6 in	=	½ ft		=	15 cm	
12 in	=	1 ft		=	30 cm	
36 in	=	3 ft	= 1 yd	=	90 cm	
40 in	=				100 cm	= 1 m

Equivalents for Different Types of Ingredients

Standard Cup	Fine Powder (ex. flour)	Grain (ex. rice)	Granular (ex. sugar)	Liquid Solids (ex. butter)	Liquid (ex. milk)
1	140 g	150 g	190 g	200 g	240 ml
¾	105 g	113 g	143 g	150 g	180 ml
⅔	93 g	100 g	125 g	133 g	160 ml
½	70 g	75 g	95 g	100 g	120 ml
⅓	47 g	50 g	63 g	67 g	80 ml
¼	35 g	38 g	48 g	50 g	60 ml
⅛	18 g	19 g	24 g	25 g	30 ml

Index

A

Appetizers
Cheesecake, Salsa, 40
Dips
Blue Cheese–Artichoke Dip, 33
Blue Cheese Dip, 36
Gruyère-Bacon Dip, 35
Cheesy–Spinach Crab Dip, 28
Roasted Garlic–White Bean
Dip, 30
Drummettes with Blue Cheese
Dip, Buffalo-Style, 36
Meatballs, Lamb, 39
Apples
Applesauce, Chunky, 226
Butter, Overnight Apple, 243
Cake, Double Apple, 264
Cider, Hot Mulled Ginger-
Spiced, 18
Cider, Spiced Caramel, 23
Oatmeal, Maple-Hazelnut, 164
Soup, Butternut Squash–
Parsnip, 196
Soup, Curried Squash and
Apple, 197
Spiced Apple Pork Chops, 87
Walnut-Stuffed Apples, 268
Apricots
Pork with Apricots, Dried Plums,
and Sauerkraut, 71
Tagine, Apricot Lamb, 102
Artichokes
Dip, Blue Cheese–Artichoke, 33
Ragout, White Bean, Artichoke,
and Chard, 191

B

Bacon
Dip, Gruyère-Bacon, 35
Green Beans, Southern-
Style, 229
Bananas Foster, Tropical, 266
Barbecue
Char Siu Pork Roast, 77
Sandwiches, Pork and Slaw, 98

Barley
Burritos, Barley, Black Bean, and
Corn, 169
Cabbage Rolls with Pine Nuts
and Currants, Barley-
Stuffed, 165
Beans
Black
Burritos, Barley, Black Bean,
and Corn, 169
Chicken Enchilada Stack, 140
Cuban Beans and Rice, 166
Feijoada, Brazilian, 62
Santa Fe Black Beans, 228
Soup, Black Bean, 187
Soup, Caribbean Black
Bean, 186
Brunswick Stew, Easy, 211
Cassoulet, Smoked
Sausage, 212
Chickpea Chili, 193
Chickpea Curry, Tofu and, 174
Chickpeas in Curried Coconut
Broth, 172
Chili, Smoky Slow-Cooked, 208
Chili, Three-Bean Vegetarian, 188
Green Beans, Southern-
Style, 229
Pinto Bean Chili with Corn and
Winter Squash, 190
Red Beans and Rice, 84
Stew, Peasant, 221
White
Cassoulet, Thyme-Scented
White Bean, 171
Chicken Supper,
Provençale, 151
Dip, Roasted Garlic–White
Bean, 30
Lamb Shanks with Cannellini
Beans, Tarragon, 109
Ragout, White Bean,
Artichoke, and Chard, 191
Soup, Tuscan Chicken, 220
Succotash, Mediterranean, 179
Tiny French Beans with
Smoked Sausage, 122
Vegetables on Couscous,
Curried, 178
Beef. *See also* **Beef, Ground; Veal.**
Brisket with Beer, Beef, 54

Burgundy with Egg Noodles,
Beef, 47
Ribs
Feijoada, Brazilian, 62
Short Ribs, Curried Beef, 53
Roasts
Pot Roast, Company, 56
Pot Roast with Turnip Greens,
Beef, 59
Provençal Beef Daube, 200
Sandwiches, Italian Beef, 49
Sauerbraten, 68
Steaks
Soup, Vegetable-Beef, 203
Stroganoff, Beef, 50
Stew, All-American Beef, 199
Thai Red Curry Beef, 66
Beef, Ground
Bolognese, 65
Meatballs in Spicy Tomato
Sauce, Moroccan, 44
Sauce with Pasta, Slow-
Simmered Meat, 61
Beets, Lemon-Rosemary, 231
Beverages
Cider, Hot Mulled Ginger-
Spiced, 18
Cider, Spiced Caramel, 23
Hot Chocolate, Mocha, 24
Hot Toddies, Ginger-Lemon, 21
Tea, Berry-Lemonade, 27
Biscuits, Vegetable Pot Pie
with Parmesan–Black
Pepper, 180
Bolognese, 65
Breads
Pudding, Brandied Plum–
Vanilla Bread, 250
Pudding, Tiramisu Bread, 246
Broth, Chickpeas in Curried
Coconut, 172
Brunswick Stew, Easy, 211
Burritos, Barley, Black Bean, and
Corn, 169
Butter, Overnight Apple, 243

C

Cabbage
Rolls, Cabbage, 93
Rolls with Pine Nuts and
Currants, Barley-Stuffed
Cabbage, 165

Slaw Sandwiches, Pork and, 98
Cacciatore, Chicken, 143

Cakes
Angel Food Cake with Mixed
Berry Compote, 257
Apple Cake, Double, 264
Brownie Pudding Cake, 263
Cheesecake, Amaretti, 259
Caramel Cider, Spiced, 23

Carrots
Chicken with Carrots and
Potatoes, 154
Honey-Orange Carrots, 230
Lamb Shanks with Cannellini
Beans, Tarragon, 109
Ragout of Veal, 115
Cassoulet, Smoked Sausage, 212
Cassoulet, Thyme-Scented White
Bean, 171
Char Siu Pork Roast, 77

Cheese
Biscuits, Vegetable Pot Pie
with Parmesan–Black
Pepper, 180
Black Beans, Santa Fe, 228
Cabbage Rolls with Pine Nuts
and Currants, Barley-
Stuffed, 165
Cheesecake, Amaretti, 259
Cheesecake, Salsa, 40
Chicken Enchilada Stack, 140
Dip, Blue Cheese, 36
Dip, Blue Cheese–Artichoke, 33
Dip, Gruyère-Bacon, 35
Dip, Cheesy–Spinach
Crab, 28
Potatoes, Loaded Twice-
Baked, 238
Soup, Potato, 185
Cherries, Turkey Thighs with Olives
and Dried, 124

Chicken
Brunswick Stew, Easy, 211
Cacciatore, Chicken, 143
Carrots and Potatoes, Chicken
with, 154
Chilaquiles, 133
Drummettes with Blue Cheese
Dip, Buffalo-Style, 36
Enchilada Stack, Chicken, 140
Fricassee, Old-Fashioned
Chicken, 158

Garlic Chicken, 131
Glazed Chicken Thighs,
Sweet, 157
Jambalaya, Chicken and
Shrimp, 149
Jambalaya, Sausage, 82
Korma, Chicken, 128
Lemon-Rosemary Chicken, 156
Mediterranean Chicken, 134
Orange-Rosemary Chicken, 127
Provençale Chicken Supper, 151
Sandwiches, Pulled Chicken, 152
Saucy Chicken over Rice, 159
Sesame-Ginger Chicken, 145
Soup, Rosemary Chicken
Noodle, 219
Soup, Tuscan Chicken, 220
Stew, Peasant, 221
Stew, Spicy Chicken, 216
Stew with Green Olives,
Chicken, 214
Sweet and Sour Chicken, 121
Verde, Chicken, 146
Chilaquiles, 133

Chili
Chickpea Chili, 193
Pinto Bean Chili with Corn and
Winter Squash, 190
Smoky Slow-Cooked Chili, 208
Three-Bean Vegetarian Chili, 188
Turkey and Hominy Chili, 223

Chocolate
Cake, Brownie Pudding, 263
Mocha Hot Chocolate, 24
Chutney, Chunky Peach-Ginger, 245
Chutney Sauce, Meatballs with, 110

Coconut
Broth, Chickpeas in Curried
Coconut, 172
Tapioca, Pineapple-Coconut, 254

Corn
Brunswick Stew, Easy, 211
Burritos, Barley, Black Bean, and
Corn, 169
Chili with Corn and Winter
Squash, Pinto Bean, 190
Pudding, Poblano Corn, 235

Couscous
Curried Vegetables on
Couscous, 178
Stuffed Peppers, Herb and
Sausage–, 161

Crab Dip, Cheesy–Spinach, 28
Curry, Indian Lamb, 107
Curry, Tofu and Chickpea, 174

D
Desserts. *See also* **Cakes,
Puddings.**
Apples, Walnut-Stuffed, 268
Bananas Foster, Tropical, 266
Custard, Vanilla Bean Baked, 252
Pears, Spiced Poached, 249
Tapioca, Pineapple-Coconut, 254

E
Eggs
Noodles, Beef Burgundy with
Egg, 47
Spanish Tortilla (*Tortilla de
Patatas*), 176
Enchilada Stack, Chicken, 140

F
Feijoada, Brazilian, 62
Fig Jam, Orange-, 242
Fricassee, Old-Fashioned
Chicken, 158
Fruit. *See also* **specific types.**
Tea, Berry-Lemonade, 27
Compote, Angel Food Cake with
Mixed Berry, 257

G
Garlic
Beef Daube, Provençal, 200
Beef Short Ribs, Curried, 53
Beef, Thai Red Curry, 66
Black Beans, Santa Fe, 228
Black-Eyed Peas, Spicy, 236
Bolognese, 65
Chicken, Garlic, 131
Chicken Korma, 128
Chicken Verde, 146
Chilaquiles, 133
Chili, Chickpea, 193
Chili, Turkey and Hominy, 223
Feijoada, Brazilian, 62
Lamb Curry, Indian, 107
Leg of Lamb, Zinfandel-
Braised, 104
Meat Sauce with Pasta, Slow-
Simmered, 61
Osso Buco with Gremolata, 112

Pork Carnitas, 81
Pork Vindaloo, 78
Posole, 205
Ratatouille, 177
Red Beans and Rice, 84
Roasted Garlic–White Bean
    Dip, 30
Sliders with Horseradish Aioli,
    Rosemary Pork, 97
Soup, Caribbean Black
    Bean, 186
Soup, Curried Lentil-Tomato, 195
Squash, Stuffed, 100
Veal Paprikash, 116
Ginger
Chicken, Sesame-Ginger, 145
Chutney, Chunky Peach-
    Ginger, 245
Cider, Hot Mulled Ginger-
    Spiced, 18
Hot Toddies, Ginger-Lemon, 21
Greens
Collard Greens, Balsamic, 233
Turnip Greens, Beef Pot Roast
    with, 59
Gremolata, Osso Buco with, 112

H

Hominy
Chili, Turkey and Hominy, 223
Posole, 205
Honey-Orange Carrots, 230
Hoppin' John, 173

J

Jambalaya
Chicken and Shrimp
    Jambalaya, 149
Sausage Jambalaya, 82
Jam, Orange-Fig, 242

K

Korma, Chicken, 128

L

Lamb
Braised Lamb with Picholine
    Olives, 105
Curry, Indian Lamb, 107
Leg of Lamb, Zinfandel-
    Braised, 104
Meatballs, Lamb, 39

Meatballs with Chutney
    Sauce, 110
Shanks with Cannellini Beans,
    Tarragon Lamb, 109
Squash, Stuffed, 100
Tagine, Apricot Lamb, 102
Tagine, Lamb, 103
Leeks
Ragout of Veal, 115
Ragout, White Bean, Artichoke,
    and Chard, 191
Lemon
Beets, Lemon-Rosemary, 231
Beverages
    Hot Toddies, Ginger-Lemon, 21
    Tea, Berry-Lemonade, 27
Chicken, Lemon-Rosemary, 156
Lentils
Soup, Curried Lentil-Tomato, 195
Soup, Smoked Turkey–Lentil, 222

M

Maple-Hazelnut Oatmeal, 164
Marinated
Beef Daube, Provencal, 200
Pork Roast, Char Siu, 77
Pot Roast, Company, 56
Sandwiches, Italian Beef, 49
Sauerbraten, 68
Meatballs
Chutney Sauce, Meatballs
    with, 110
Lamb Meatballs, 39
Moroccan Meatballs in Spicy
    Tomato Sauce, 44
Meatless sausage
Cassoulet, Thyme-Scented White
    Bean, 171
Mushrooms
Beef Burgundy with Egg
    Noodles, 47
Beef Stroganoff, 50
Chicken Cacciatore, 143

N

Noodles
Egg Noodles, Beef Burgundy
    with, 47
Garlic-Sauced Noodles, Chinese
    Pork Tenderloin with, 90
Soup, Rosemary Chicken
    Noodle, 219

O

Oatmeal, Maple-Hazelnut, 164
Olives
Chicken, Mediterranean, 134
Chili, Chickpea, 193
Lamb with Picholine Olives,
    Braised, 105
Stew with Green Olives,
    Chicken, 214
Succotash, Mediterranean, 179
Turkey, Mediterranean Roast, 126
Turkey Thighs with Olives and
    Dried Cherries, 124
Onions
Beef Brisket with Beer, 54
Beef, Thai Red Curry, 66
Black Beans, Santa Fe, 228
Cabbage Rolls, 93
Collard Greens, Balsamic, 233
Dip, Blue Cheese-Artichoke, 33
Feijoada, Brazilian, 62
Lamb with Picholine Olives,
    Braised, 105
Pork Chops, Spiced Apple, 87
Pork Vindaloo, 78
Sauerbraten, 68
Soup, Black Bean, 187
Tagine, Apricot Lamb, 102
Tagine, Lamb, 103
Turkey, Sweet and Spicy
    Satsuma, 137
Oranges
Carrots, Honey-Orange, 230
Chicken, Orange-Rosemary, 127
Jam, Orange-Fig, 242
Turkey, Sweet and Spicy
    Satsuma, 137
Osso Buco with Gremolata, 112

P

Parsnips
Beef Brisket with Beer, 54
Soup, Butternut Squash–
    Parsnip, 196
Pasta, Slow-Simmered Meat Sauce
    with, 61
Peach-Ginger Chutney, Chunky, 245
Peanut
Chinese Pork Tenderloin with
    Garlic-Sauced Noodles, 90
Pork, Caribbean-Style, 89
Stew, Thai-Style Pork, 206

Pears, Spiced Poached, 249

Peas
Black-Eyed
Hoppin' John, 173
Spicy Black-Eyed Peas, 236

Peppers
Beans and Rice, Cuban, 166
Black-Eyed Peas, Spicy, 236
Cheesecake, Salsa, 40
Chicken Cacciatore, 143
Chicken, Sweet and Sour, 121
Chicken Verde, 146
Chilaquiles, 133
Poblano Corn Pudding, 235
Pork, Caribbean-Style, 89
Sandwiches, Italian Beef, 49
Soup, Caribbean Black
Bean, 186
Stew, Thai-Style Pork, 206
Stuffed Peppers, Herb and
Sausage–, 161
Pie with Parmesan–Black Pepper
Biscuits, Vegetable Pot, 180

Pineapple
Bananas Foster, Tropical, 266
Chicken, Sweet and Sour, 121
Chicken Thighs, Sweet
Glazed, 157
Tapioca, Pineapple-Coconut, 254

Plums
Bread Pudding, Brandied Plum–
Vanilla, 250
Lamb Tagine, 103
Pork Loin with Port and Dried
Plums, Braised, 94
Pork Tenderloin, Plum, 72
Pork with Apricots, Dried Plums,
and Sauerkraut, 71

Pork. *See also* **Bacon, Sausage.**
Bolognese, 65
Brunswick Stew, Easy, 211
Cabbage Rolls, 93
Carnitas, Pork, 81
Chili, Smoky Slow-Cooked, 208
Chops, Spiced Apple Pork, 87
Curried Pork over Basmati
Rice, 75
Feijoada, Brazilian, 62
Roasts
Braised Pork Loin with Port
and Dried Plums, 94
Caribbean-Style Pork, 89

Cassoulet, Smoked
Sausage, 212
Char Siu Pork Roast, 77
Sandwiches, Pork and
Slaw, 98
Sliders with Horseradish Aioli,
Rosemary Pork, 97
Vindaloo, Pork, 78
Stew, Thai-Style Pork, 206
Tenderloin
Apricots, Dried Plums, and
Sauerkraut, Pork with, 71
Chinese Pork Tenderloin with
Garlic-Sauced Noodles, 90
Plum Pork Tenderloin, 72
Posole, 205

Potatoes. *See also* **Sweet Potato.**
Brunswick Stew, Easy, 211
Chicken Korma, 128
Chicken with Carrots and
Potatoes, 154
Loaded Twice-Baked
Potatoes, 238
Pork over Basmati Rice,
Curried, 75
Soup, Potato, 185
Spanish Tortilla (*Tortilla de
Patatas*), 176

Puddings
Bread
Plum–Vanilla Bread Pudding,
Brandied, 250
Tiramisu Bread Pudding, 246
Brownie Pudding Cake, 263
Corn Pudding, Poblano, 235
Rum-Raisin Arborio Pudding, 260

R
Ragout of Veal, 115
Ragout, White Bean, Artichoke, and
Chard, 191
Ratatouille, 177

Rice
Basmati Rice, Curried Pork
over, 75
Beans and Rice, Cuban, 166
Pudding, Rum-Raisin
Arborio, 260
Red Beans and Rice, 84
Saucy Chicken over Rice, 159

S
Salsa Cheesecake, 40

Sandwiches
Beef Sandwiches, Italian, 49
Pork and Slaw Sandwiches, 98
Pulled Chicken Sandwiches, 152
Sliders with Horseradish Aioli,
Rosemary Pork, 97

Sauces
Bolognese, 65
Chutney Sauce, Meatballs
with, 110
Meat Sauce with Pasta, Slow-
Simmered, 61
Tomato Sauce, Moroccan
Meatballs in Spicy, 44
Sauerbraten, 68

Sauerkraut
Cabbage Rolls, 93
Pork with Apricots, Dried Plums,
and Sauerkraut, 71

Sausage
Cabbage Rolls, 93
Jambalaya, Chicken and
Shrimp, 149
Jambalaya, Sausage, 82
Peppers, Herb and Sausage–
Stuffed, 161
Red Beans and Rice, 84
Sauce with Pasta, Slow-
Simmered Meat, 61
Smoked Sausage Cassoulet, 212
Smoked Sausage, Tiny French
Beans with, 122
Sesame-Ginger Chicken, 145

Shrimp
Jambalaya, Chicken and
Shrimp, 149
Jambalaya, Sausage, 82

Soups. *See also* **Stews.**
Black Bean Soup, 187
Black Bean Soup,
Caribbean, 186
Butternut Squash–Parsnip
Soup, 196
Chicken Noodle Soup,
Rosemary, 219
Chicken Soup, Tuscan, 220
Lentil-Tomato Soup, Curried, 195
Posole, 205
Potato Soup, 185
Smoked Turkey–Lentil Soup, 222

Squash and Apple Soup,
Curried, 197
Vegetable-Beef Soup, 203
Spinach
Beef, Thai Red Curry, 66
Dip, Cheesy–Spinach
Crab, 28
Soup, Tuscan Chicken, 220
Spreads
Apple Butter, Overnight, 243
Horseradish Aioli, Rosemary Pork
Sliders with, 97
Squash
Butternut
Chili, Chickpea, 193
Chili with Corn and Winter
Squash, Pinto Bean, 190
Soup, Butternut Squash–
Parsnip, 196
Soup, Curried Squash and
Apple, 197
Stuffed Squash, 100
Stews
Apricot Lamb Tagine, 102
Beef Stew, All-American, 199
Brunswick Stew, Easy, 211
Chicken Fricassee, Old-
Fashioned, 158
Chicken Stew, Spicy, 216
Chicken Stew with Green
Olives, 214
Feijoada, Brazilian, 62
Lamb Tagine, 103
Peasant Stew, 221
Pork Stew, Thai-Style, 206
Stroganoff, Beef, 50
Succotash, Mediterranean, 179
Sweet and Sour Chicken, 121
Sweet Potato Gratin, 241
Swiss Chard
Ragout, White Bean, Artichoke,
and Chard, 191

T

Tagine, Apricot Lamb, 102
Tagine, Lamb, 103
Tofu and Chickpea Curry, 174
Tomatillos
Chicken Verde, 146

Tomatoes
Cassoulet, Thyme-Scented White
Bean, 171
Chicken Enchilada Stack, 140
Chicken, Mediterranean, 134
Chicken over Rice, Saucy, 159
Chicken Supper, Provençale, 151
Chickpeas in Curried Coconut
Broth, 172
Chilaquiles, 133
Chili, Three-Bean Vegetarian, 188
Chili, Turkey and Hominy, 223
Hoppin' John, 173
Indian Lamb Curry, 107
Lamb Shanks with Cannellini
Beans, Tarragon, 109
Pork Vindaloo, 78
Sauces
Bolognese, 65
Slow-Simmered Meat Sauce
with Pasta, 61
Spicy Tomato Sauce,
Moroccan Meatballs in, 44
Soup, Curried Lentil-Tomato, 195
Squash, Stuffed, 100
Stew with Green Olives,
Chicken, 214
Tortillas
Pork Carnitas, 81
Spanish Tortilla (*Tortilla de
Patatas*), 176
Stew, Spicy Chicken, 216
Turkey
Black-Eyed Peas, Spicy, 236
Braised Turkey and Asian
Vegetables, 138
Chili, Turkey and Hominy, 223
Meatballs, Lamb, 39
Olives and Dried Cherries, Turkey
Thighs with, 124
Roast Turkey, Mediterranean, 126
Satsuma Turkey, Sweet and
Spicy, 137
Soup, Smoked Turkey–Lentil, 222

V

Vanilla
Bread Pudding, Brandied Plum–
Vanilla, 250
Custard, Vanilla Bean Baked, 252

Veal
Bolognese, 65
Osso Buco with Gremolata, 112
Paprikash, Veal, 116
Ragout of Veal, 115
Vegetables. *See also* **specific types.**
Beef Burgundy with Egg
Noodles, 47
Beef Pot Roast with Turnip
Greens, 59
Braised Turkey and Asian
Vegetables, 138
Cassoulet, Thyme-Scented White
Bean, 171
Chicken Cacciatore, 143
Chicken Korma, 128
Chili, Smoky Slow-Cooked, 208
Curried Vegetables on
Couscous, 178
Pork Loin with Port and Dried
Plums, Braised, 94
Pork over Basmati Rice,
Curried, 75
Pot Pie with Parmesan–Black
Pepper Biscuits,
Vegetable, 180
Pot Roast, Company, 56
Ratatouille, 177
Soup, Rosemary Chicken
Noodle, 219
Soup, Vegetable-Beef, 203
Stew, All-American Beef, 199
Stew, Spicy Chicken, 216
Succotash, Mediterranean, 179
Veal Paprikash, 116
Vindaloo, Pork, 78

W

Walnuts
Apples, Walnut-Stuffed, 268
Cake, Brownie Pudding, 263